TEACHING HISTORY
IN THE JUNIOR SCHOOL

BY R. J. UNSTEAD

LOOKING AT HISTORY

1. FROM CAVEMEN TO VIKINGS
2. THE MIDDLE AGES
3. TUDORS AND STUARTS
4. QUEEN ANNE TO QUEEN
   ELIZABETH II

PEOPLE IN HISTORY

1. FROM CARACTACUS TO ALFRED
2. FROM WILLIAM THE CONQUEROR
   TO WILLIAM CAXTON
3. GREAT TUDORS AND STUARTS
4. GREAT PEOPLE OF MODERN TIMES

A HISTORY OF BRITAIN

1. THE MEDIEVAL SCENE 787–1485
2. CROWN AND PARLIAMENT 1485–1688
3. THE RISE OF GREAT BRITAIN 1688–1837
4. A CENTURY OF CHANGE 1837–TODAY
5. BRITAIN IN THE 20TH CENTURY

MEN AND WOMEN IN HISTORY

1. HEROES AND SAINTS
2. PRINCES AND REBELS
3. DISCOVERERS AND ADVENTURERS
4. GREAT LEADERS

LOOKING AT ANCIENT HISTORY

EARLY TIMES

Black's Junior Reference Books

A HISTORY OF HOUSES
TRAVEL BY ROAD
MONASTERIES

ST. MARTIN AND THE BEGGAR.
A "stained glass" window made by backward 9-year-olds.

TEACHING HISTORY
IN THE
JUNIOR SCHOOL

R. J. UNSTEAD

AUTHOR OF "LOOKING AT HISTORY"
"LOOKING AT ANCIENT HISTORY"
"PEOPLE IN HISTORY"
"A HISTORY OF BRITAIN" ETC.

WITH 12 ILLUSTRATIONS FROM
PHOTOGRAPHS AND 5 LINE DRAWINGS

THIRD EDITION

A. & C. BLACK LTD
LONDON

FIRST PUBLISHED IN 1956

SECOND EDITION 1959

THIRD EDITION 1963

REPRINTED WITH CORRECTIONS 1965 AND 1967

SBN: 7136   0802   1

PRINTED IN GREAT BRITAIN BY

J. W. ARROWSMITH LTD., WINTERSTOKE ROAD, BRISTOL 3.

Contents

PART I

INTRODUCTION

PART II

A JUNIOR SCHOOL SYLLABUS

PART III

HISTORY IN THE CLASSROOM

History in the Classroom, continued.

Illustrations

Introduction

THIS is a book about history in the Junior School. It has not been written for the specialist or even for the enthusiast, to whom it will appear both simple and obvious, nor does it try to expound how history *ought* to be taught. It suggests to students and to teachers who may have no special interest or knowledge of the subject various ways in which history may be made interesting and worth while for junior children.

There are, of course, few history specialists in junior schools, but there are a great many enthusiasts, who very properly have their own views about teaching history. Since they are enthusiasts, it is almost certain that they succeed in helping children to like and understand history. But, in addition to those who merely endure the subject, there is probably a host of 'general practitioners' in primary schools who enjoy history and recognize its appeal to children, but whose busy lives, with one subject following another all day, leave them little time to plan their history lessons as fully as they would wish. For them, in particular, it is hoped that this book will offer a straightforward 'plan of campaign' with some suggestions for carrying it out.

There is no royal road to teaching history, for it is a difficult, and perhaps by nature, an adult subject, so that it has sometimes been doubted whether it should be included on the school timetable at all. As far as most schools are concerned, history is a comparatively new subject, though in a desiccated form it seems to have appeared in the curriculum of 'British' schools as long ago as 1856. The notorious payment-by-results system soon stifled this liberalism and it was not until the turn of the century that history edged its way on to the timetable. From that time onwards, there seems to have been an almost universal agreement that two half-hour or forty-five-minute periods should be devoted to the subject in every type of school, even if history is sometimes disguised behind such labels as 'social studies', 'civics' or 'centres of interest'.

WHY TEACH HISTORY AT ALL?

Since teachers in primary schools habitually devote their time and energies so regularly to teaching history, it is reasonable to suppose that there is some faith in the subject and that there are reasons for teaching it. When considering planning a scheme of work for juniors, it might be worth while to examine those reasons.

An unconventional reason for teaching history was given by Professor Galbraith to a gathering of history teachers at Oxford in 1955, when he said,

'History, of course, is a vested interest like the football pools and the breweries. I make my living from it and you make your living from it!'

The Regius Professor of Modern History then went on to doubt if the intellectual discipline of history was as exacting, as precise or as easily examined as the discipline of, say, classics or mathematics.

Why, indeed, teach history at all?

Taxed with the question, many teachers may well feel that while it is right and proper to include history on the timetable, there is little point in indulging in philosophical speculation about its value. Pressed further, however, they might admit that there is something in what the Ministry of Education Pamphlet No. 23 says, when it remarks,

'In England, as in other countries, it has been the general feeling over the centuries that to ignore the experience of the past is not merely folly, but a sort of impiety.'

In other words, they teach history for two main reasons; firstly for what may be called moral values, and secondly, for its power to enrich the minds and imaginations of children.

However daunting it may sound nowadays to speak of moral

values, a great many folk still believe that honesty and courage, mercy and loyalty are cardinal virtues. And they think that our children are more likely to grow into citizens of the kind of race that, in our better moments, we know ourselves to be, if they have been made aware of the qualities of men and women whom successive generations have admired.

It is not too much to say that the true glory of immortality is not renown through the centuries, but its formative power upon a nation's children.

The courage of Scott and Drake, the tenacity of Bruce and Churchill, the compassion of Barnardo, Elizabeth Fry and Shaftesbury, the persistence and faith of Bunyan and the Pilgrim Fathers are moral qualities which we put before children in the belief that they will impress themselves upon those undeveloped personalities as the standards of conduct to which people may at least aspire.

Trevelyan has said,

'There is no utilitarian value in knowledge of the past and there is no way of scientifically deducing causal laws from the actions of human beings in the mass. In short, the value of history is not scientific. Its true value is educational. It can educate the minds of men by causing them to reflect upon the past.'

One is aware, of course, that there has been a reaction against the heroic presentation of history. The debunkers can show that Richard I, hero of every schoolboy, was no better than a swaggering bully who treated his social inferiors with revolting barbarity; Bruce, they may continue, was a murderer, Montrose a traitor and Marlborough an avaricious place-seeker. The same technique and scepticism of the nature of greatness have recently been applied to the reputations of T. E. Lawrence and Wingate of Burma.

But debunking is a sterile occupation. While observing moderation in hero-worship, there are still those who retain an old-fashioned conviction that the examples of great men and women have a fundamental value in teaching history to children.

While it is possible to over-emphasize the Great Men of History, there is a fashionable tendency to over-stress the 'Little Men', as if

3

all history can be presented in terms of the ordinary man's struggle for food and shelter.

A second prime reason for teaching history to juniors lies in its power to enrich their imaginations. Junior children are interested in people—in how they live, work and amuse themselves, whether they are Eskimos, Arabs or medieval villeins. A child's lack of experience and of preconceived ideas is an asset, for he can enter into the life of the Lake Village or Manor with the same ease and gusto that permits him, in his unsophisticated games, to transform a collection of old tins and planks into an Indian encampment or a space-rocket. Moreover, to a young child's literal mind, people in history have the special fascination that they were 'real' and their stories are true.

MUST HISTORY BE DULL?

The driest thing that the Mouse could think of when the bedraggled company assembled at the edge of Alice's Pool of Tears was history. That is the traditional view of history. Only the memory of its excruciating dullness at school could have produced the howls of uproarious delight that greeted and have gone on greeting that masterpiece *1066 And All That*.

The dates, battles, kings and causes that were to have been committed to memory by a couple of generations went into the making of the glorious muddle and the cascade of howlers that fill that celebrated book. We should be grateful that cramming 'inert ideas' into children has had at least this one glorious result.

Yet it is only school history which is considered dull by the general public, who do not at all accept Henry Ford's dictum 'History is bunk!' As J. Hampden Jackson has pointed out, they have a passion for history when it is presented to them in the brilliance of so many historical films, or as biography or televised drama. Not all these films and plays and books about the 'olden days' are good history, nor are they all bad, but they appeal to the imagination and love of actuality of a public which is not so different from its children in school. Somewhere, between the glamorous inaccuracies of

4

Hollywood and the arid facts of the academic textbooks lies a means of making history both enjoyable and educational.

THE LEGACY OF 'DULLNESS'

Recently, when the author asked a number of young teachers for their views on history, all but one confessed that the subject was unspeakably boring and all agreed that they had felt ill-equipped to teach it when they left Training College. At about the same time, a college principal remarked that the weakest subject that his students brought to college was history and, generally speaking, they found great difficulty in teaching it during their school practice.

These young people had all attended grammar schools and it is significant that history became increasingly unpalatable to them as they neared their G.C.E. examination at Ordinary level.

That teachers of history in grammar schools deplore the cramping effect of the examination is evident from a report in *The Times Educational Supplement*:

'the teachers . . . pointed out the disservice the [G.C.E.] examination seems to do to the subject, the cold facts that must be assimilated unquestioningly from the textbook, and the lessons which must be ruled by the strict demands of the examination syllabus. Where notes dictated by the teacher are such an effective way of teaching the requisite dates, battles and causes, it seems that the best results invite the worst methods, and the teachers spoke feelingly of the number of intelligent children who must be turned against history for life by this one gruelling experience.'

Thus, it seems that an examination taken by nearly all future teachers calls, of necessity, for dull and uninspired teaching of material which, in itself, is often unrelated to the pupil's experience, or indeed to anything else within the syllabus itself. While there is undoubtedly a great deal of very good history teaching in grammar schools, it is still broadly true that the traditional dullness caused by the examination system projects its influence into the primary school by giving many young teachers an attitude to the subject which is quite out of keeping with the needs of young children, and from which the inexperienced teacher must try to recover.

THE YOUNG TEACHER'S READJUSTMENT OF OUTLOOK

The young teacher in a junior school will almost always be teaching history as well as, *inter alia*, English, arithmetic, geography, scripture and nature study, and she will be unusually fortunate if she does not start with this legacy of a cramped and ill-digested history course.

For several years, she will have concentrated upon a narrow and academic view of history, usually much concerned with causes, wars, movements and political changes. At college, during a three-year course, occupying just over 100 weeks, from which school practice, examinations, half-terms and specialization have to be deducted, she will have been fortunate if she has attended as many as 70 one-hour periods devoted, not merely to history, but also to some consideration of teaching the subject.

In view of these circumstances, it is surprising that some Training Colleges still devote a high proportion of their slender time to the nineteenth century, which is about the one period which students will almost certainly have 'done', or to a rapid survey of the civilizations of the Ancient World, though there is far more to be said for this latter.

Yet, in her first term, a young teacher may find herself expected to teach seven- and eight-year-olds about Cave Men or Romans, and, a year later, she may be teaching nine-year-olds about medieval England. She will protest that she has not 'done' these periods of history since her first or second forms at grammar school, and the stories of Caractacus and Caxton have faded from her memory under the remorseless pressure of later examinations. Worse, she may find herself enmeshed in one of those concentric schemes which compel her to range from Caesar to Churchill, from Boadicea to J. L. Baird during each junior year, with excursions into world history to recount the achievements of Hammurabi, Dante, Galileo and George Washington!

6

How is a young teacher, or indeed any teacher, to cope with this kind of situation, if she wishes to do more than keep one chapter ahead of the class and also tries to answer those vital questions 'Is it true?' and 'How do we know?'

The teacher of juniors who hopes to teach history effectively must recapture, or discover perhaps for the first time, an enjoyment of history as the story of human beings, and she will need, firstly, some feeling and understanding of the broad currents of history, rather than a knowledge of political causes and economic consequences. It is therefore encouraging that there seems to be an increasing tendency for Training Colleges to provide an outline survey of history for students taking it as an ordinary subject.

While such an outline may be dubbed superficial, limitations of time at college can rarely provide a better alternative course, and it seems important that the student should try to achieve a panoramic view of, at least, British history, though there will be no general agreement that this is the prime concern of the junior school. If the student gains a conception of the stream of time that is history—and it is all too easy to take for granted that she does possess this time-chart of the mind—she will at least have achieved some realization of the continuity of history.

It is not suggested that junior children should make a regular practice of concocting time-charts, showing rulers, leaders, writers, main events and dynasties, together with borders depicting furniture, food, houses and vehicles, but it is suggested, in all diffidence, that students in Training College could be much worse employed than performing such an exercise, which might at least give them an idea of when men worshipped at Stonehenge, or wore the capuchon, or sat on Hepplewhite chairs for the first time.

A TEACHER'S READING

Probably the most important impression that Training Colleges can implant into the minds of students is that they have not finished acquiring knowledge when they leave to take up their first posts in schools, for the world of scholarship is not likely to have been conquered after two or three years at college.

In no field is this more true than history. No one would suggest that young teachers should shut themselves away in a study every evening and week-end, when they might be following various unacademic activities, but from time to time, they ought to make some effort to acquire the background knowledge which is needed to teach history, if only for an hour a week to nine-year-olds.

At a later stage in this book, there are some book-lists which may help teachers who are not familiar with many common and easily obtained sources of historical information, but it may be worth remarking here that every junior school should contain in its staffroom or library at least some of the following books:

Quennell: *Everyday Life in Prehistoric Times; Everyday Life in Roman Britain; Everyday Life in Anglo-Saxon, Viking and Norman Times; A History of Everyday Things in England* (4 vols. Batsford).
Mitchell & Leys: *A History of the English People* (Longmans).
Trevelyan: *Illustrated English Social History* (Longmans).
Oxford Junior Encyclopaedia (O.U.P.).
Unstead: *Looking at Ancient History* (Black).
Unstead: *Looking at History* (Black)
Unstead: *England* (Black).
How They Lived series (Blackwell).

Source Material

In addition to the list above, which may be taken as an irreducible minimum and to which a score of titles howl for inclusion, the nonspecialist teacher may wish, from time to time, to find out, or to help his children to discover, exactly what people said or did at some particular moment of the past. From an enormous list, one might select the following books from which extracts interesting to older juniors may be taken:

Picture Source Books for Social History (Allen and Unwin).
They Saw It Happen (4 vols. Blackwell).
Documents of English History (2 vols. Black).
Dover Wilson: *Life in Shakespeare's England* (Penguin).
Reference Books to Macmillan's History Class Pictures. *Texts for*

Students (Sheldon Press) esp. 'Village Life in the Fifteenth Century'; 'Sports and Pastimes in the Middle Ages'; 'Travellers and Travelling in the Middle Ages'.

The Anglo-Saxon Chronicle, *Pepys's Diary*, *Captain Cook's Voyages*, *Dorothy Osborne's Letters*, *Hakluyt's Voyages* (Everyman Library, Dent), *A.D. News Sheets* (Allen & Unwin), *Jackdaw* series (Cape).

From sources such as these, children can hear exactly what happened when Cook's ship went aground on the Great Barrier Reef, or the very words which the 'prentice used to cajole customers—

'Will ye buy a fine cabinet, a fine scarf, or a rich girdle and hangers? See here, madam, fine cobweb lawn good cambric, or fair bone lace. Will ye buy any very fine silk stocks, sir? See here a fair hat of the French block, sir. What do ye lack, do ye buy, sir, see what ye lack? Pins, points, garters, Spanish gloves or silk ribbons?'

They may read perhaps how the French Ambassador described the great Queen Elizabeth in 1597, that Pepys paid 4*d.* for opening the vein of his maid, 'being sick', or that a schoolmaster in 1629 'must be a man of sound religion, neither Papist nor Puritan, of a grave behaviour, and sober and honest conversation, no tippler or haunter of ale-houses, and no puffer of tabacco.'

PART II

A Junior School Syllabus

WHAT HISTORY SHALL WE TEACH TO JUNIORS?

WHEN considering the content of a history syllabus in the junior school, it may be well to ask the following questions:

(i) What are the interests and characteristics of junior children?

(ii) What history can juniors understand?

(iii) What will interest them—bearing in mind the fact that history abounds with apocryphal anecdotes and splendidly blood-thirsty events which may be attractive but historically unsound?

(iv) Should history in the primary school be regarded as a foundation upon which subsequent knowledge and interest will be built?

Answering the first question may well provide the answers to the greater part of the others. Most teachers agree that, as far as one dare generalize, children between seven and twelve years are eager and inquisitive, loving to find out things for themselves if they are given a lead, though their powers of concentration are usually short. They are busy, active and industrious so long as their interest is held, but they deal un-self-critically with broad effects and slapdash finish, rather than with minute detail and meticulous precision. Yet, they are often eager for exact answers to 'How did it work?' and 'Why did they do that?' For them, lacking experience, the world is still a personal affair, measured in sharp outlines, black and white, good and bad. Nevertheless, they have an acute awareness of, for example, fear and hunger and cold, which made up so much of the Cave Man's life, but abstract ideas, causes and effects are boring because they lie outside personal experience. Most juniors have an enormous appetite for romance and a keen dramatic sense, under a teacher who has the faintest interest in acting.

With these characteristics in mind, a teacher will at once reject political history and he will view with distrust schemes based upon an abstraction like 'Freedom' and even those popular studies of 'Transport', 'Clothes' or 'Homes' if they seem to lend undue bias to materialistic things. Inevitably, he will conclude that history, for juniors, must deal with people.

It is of course true that history, in almost any form, must be the story of people through the ages, but this does not always seem apparent to young people when emphasis has to be laid upon political and economic movements. Causes of wars, social changes, laws, institutions and alliances are the activities of men and women, but juniors are not interested in generalizations or in analyses of human conduct. They want to hear about particular men and women, what they did, how they lived, worked and amused themselves.

In short, history in the junior school will be concerned with People and How They Lived.

SOME PROBLEMS OF PLANNING A JUNIOR COURSE

If there is agreement that the chief concern of the history lesson will be with people, the question then arises, 'Which people?'

There is a liberal school of thought which deplores concentration upon British history alone. This point of view, which has much to commend it, holds that we shall deprive children of their cultural heritage if we do not put before them the classical stories of the Ancient World and the great figures of European and world history. Can we, in the name of education, deny them the stories of Achilles and Alexander, of Marco Polo, St. Francis, Joan of Arc, Leonardo and Abraham Lincoln?

Yet if we accept this persuasive view, the teacher in the classroom will cry even more loudly than usual, 'But I can never cover the syllabus!'

After all, there are only four years, of barely forty weeks each, in the junior child's school life and it will be surprising if history occupies more than one hour a week during that time, especially if it is thought of as a 'subject'. Does it mean then that we shall be forced to choose Garibaldi and ignore Charles Edward Stuart? Shall we find ourselves compelled to remove Caxton from the syllabus in order to make room for Galileo?

Fortunately, the problem need hardly arise. History is not a water-tight compartment and the importance of linking history with English is so obvious that there is no need to labour the point. Literature is as much concerned with people as is history, and surely the English course will include some of the great classical legends and world-famous stories? It will be surprising if the class libraries do not contain such stories as 'He went with Columbus' and 'Marco Polo'. It does not require very much ingenuity to introduce such great figures of world history as Joan of Arc, St. Francis and Albert Schweitzer into the English, 'comprehension' and Scripture lessons.

Furthermore, children are not concluding their study of history in the junior school. Most secondary schools study the Ancient World in some detail, while world history, in one form or another, almost always plays an important part in a secondary syllabus.

THE HISTORY OF OUR OWN PEOPLE

Even at the risk of being thought parochial, teachers of juniors will do well to confine the bulk of their teaching to British history —that is to say, the story of the people from whom we have sprung and who were our ancestors; the people who, in some ways, re-sembled us. But we must be very careful not to present them as 'people just like us', because for a great part of our history they thought and behaved differently, and it is essential that we never pretend that the Pastons and Tudors, apart from their fancy dress, were just like your father and mine. It is equally important to preserve children from the view that our ancestors were undersized, rather stupid and superstitious folk who had not yet received the benefits of modern progress.

THE PROBLEM OF CHRONOLOGY

It has become almost axiomatic to say that junior children have no chronological sense. It is certainly true that for younger children, grandma's day is as remote as Boadicea's. Most adults have been asked, 'When you were a little boy, was it the Middle Ages?' or 'Mummy, what was it like in the "olden days"?'

Yet, because young children lack a developed chronological sense for most of the time that they are juniors, that is no reason to pretend that chronology itself does not exist.

History is a process of time. It is a sequence, a stream of events, a continuous story, and it is folly to present it as anything else.

It used to be fashionable, in certain quarters, to advocate teaching history backwards. The theory was that children started from some familiar point of interest and delved backwards into the past. Possibly, in the hands of a teacher who believed in it, the scheme had advantages, but it is difficult to think of a way of teaching history that could be more confusing.

Far more common in the junior school is the syllabus based upon 'concentric' history. One popular and lavish series of history textbooks contains biographies that range from Hammurabi and Alexander to Galileo, Nelson and Baird, all for nine-year-olds. Another, written in a tone suitable for from eight to ten years, ranges from Red Erik and Mohammed to de Lesseps and General Gordon. Even more remarkable are those able and widely purchased series of history books which follow a plan of skipping across the centuries four times in four years.

Here, in detail, are the contents of one such series, containing a large number of admirably written stories:

Book 1. Stories of the Ancient World.

Book 2. Caractacus, St. Alban, Hengist and Horsa, Gregory, Alfred, Duke Rolf, Wulfstan, Edward I, Caxton, Gilbert, The *Mayflower*, James Watt, Crompton, Nelson, and Florence Nightingale.

Book 3. Boadicea, St. Patrick, St. Columba, Canute, William I,

Richard I, John, Llewellyn, Bruce, Edward III, Richard II, Cabot, More, Drake, James I, East India Company, William Penn, James Wolfe, Wellington, Grey, Allenby, Roosevelt.

Book 4. Agricola, Edwin, Bede, Dunstan, Edward the Confessor, Becket, de Montfort, Wycliffe, Wolsey, Raleigh, Charles I, Anne, Clive, Pitt, Shaftesbury, Disraeli and Gladstone.

Now, it is true that these stories are very well told, and it is possible to see that they were chosen according to a plan. They certainly are not haphazard, and one can almost imagine the author and publisher saying,

'We shall go over British history three times in the last three years of the junior course, selecting suitable stories and increasing the vocabulary-difficulty with each book. Children love stories, and these are good stories, simply and accurately told.'

Yet, how can this method of presenting history lead to anything but confusion? Although the sense of sequence is not abandoned, it is very much weakened by going over 2,000 years of history three times in three years (four times in other similar series). The lack of time-sense and the chronological confusions so common among older children and adults may well originate from this unhistorical method of presenting history.

This is by no means to make a plea for the hammering home of dates, nor for time-charts in the junior school. Indeed, it is noticeable that this unchronological treatment of history leads to those winding serpents with archbishops and soldiers standing upon their appropriate dates, usually on the end-papers of the textbooks. The stories themselves suffer, for it becomes necessary to introduce explanatory asides as to how it is that we have jumped from thirteenth-century Venice into fourteenth-century Canterbury. The background for each story has to be sketched in at the start, which usually means a disconnected and, to juniors, a boring paragraph before the story can get under way. In one case, a story about Will Shakespeare requires several pages of introductory description of Elizabethan London before the Bard makes his appearance. The real

14

point is that if the scheme hurries across time so quickly and frequently, there is no time to build up an understanding of a period.

Some simple and quite unscientific tests carried out by the author in his own school suggest that, by ten and eleven years, children are beginning to develop a considerable chronological sense. A ten-to eleven-year-old class ('A' stream) was given several groups of people, events and pictures and was asked to arrange them in historical sequence. The groups included invasions (Saxons, Romans, Danes, Normans), battles (Waterloo, Culloden, Hastings, Armada), queens (Anne, Elizabeth, Philippa, Victoria), sailors (Nelson, Drake, Cook), soldiers (William I, Wellington, Marlborough, Black Prince) &c. and there were pictures of houses, weapons, vehicles and clothes. The boys in this class averaged 83 per cent. correct and the girls 70 per cent. If it is thought that the test was very easy, one suggests that it is tried upon adults or even upon young student teachers!

A FOUR-YEAR SYLLABUS FOR JUNIORS

The suggestions below for a junior school course comprise a very simple and straightforward, even an obvious, scheme.

First Year: seven- and eight-year-olds learn how our first ancestors lived, from Early Man in the Stone, Bronze and Iron Ages to the Ancient Britons, then the Roman Occupation and the Saxon and Danish invasions.

Thus the first year is concerned with pre-history and early times until 1066.

Second Year: What used to be called 'Standard Two', interests itself in the Middle Ages, from the Norman Conquest until the time of Caxton.

Third Year: nine- and ten-year-olds devote their year to studying the Tudor and Stuart period.

Fourth Year: Top-year juniors investigate certain aspects of the Georgian and Victorian eras, with some topics, such as cars and aeroplanes, that carry them to the present day.*

* See Appendix IV for a modified syllabus for one- and two-teacher schools.

This scheme has certain advantages. It is chronological and straightforward, both for children and teachers. It is chronological without having to stress dates, for stories of men and women within their periods can be introduced naturally and without descriptive preamble, since the children will be already, to some extent, immersed in the period. The story, for instance, of how Master Chaucer went to Canterbury, will be more readily understood and remembered because it will be told to children already familiar with monasteries, pilgrims and the perils of travel along medieval roads.

Instead of careering across the centuries, picking out here a character and there an incident, there will be opportunity throughout a whole year to discover a period of history in some detail, and for young children to begin to understand the way of life during that time. This will not only facilitate the making of models, friezes and booklets, but will encourage activities which naturally arise out of an interest built up over weeks and months. Throughout the year, children are far more likely to bring along pictures, models and scraps of information from their reading, listening and 'viewing' than if their history teaching is no more than a superficial canter across widely different periods.

But it may be objected that, while this suggestion for an obviously chronological scheme pays regard to the views of those who favour the 'patch' or 'topic' methods of teaching history, it ignores the approach usually called 'lines of development'.

This method consists of selecting certain topics, such as 'Food', 'Transport', 'Houses', and tracing their development through successive centuries. The advantages are clearly that children are studying everyday things which are particularly interesting to them, such as their homes, the new housing estate, the local railway station, aeroplanes; there will be things to see, places to visit and the topic will have bearing upon much of the work done in other subjects. Moreover, there are many excellent school books to help these studies, and teachers find that children are given a strong incentive to search out information for themselves and to record it effectively. Thoughtful people feel that this approach helps to break down barriers which have arisen between subjects on the timetable, and that it provides children with an attitude of enquiry which is more important than precise knowledge.

In the hands of a gifted and enthusiastic teacher, there is no doubt that much valuable work is done along 'lines of development' and no useful history scheme can afford to ignore them. But, in the junior school, the method may have serious defects. Used unimaginatively, it can lead to a laboured correlation of subjects and, worse, to a disastrous narrowing of interest as far as history is concerned. The age of Elizabeth, for instance, can come to mean no more than the time when coaches came into use in England, or, as has been pointed out elsewhere, children can become more concerned with the great Queen's head-dress than with what went on inside that head and about her person. There develops a tendency to dwell upon things—chain mail, wimples, solars and steam-carriages—rather than upon the people who used them. Finally, it is surely slightly absurd for young children in the junior school to be tracing the development of 'things' through the ages, when they have not learned much if anything about the lives and behaviour of people in those times.

A FOUR-YEAR SYLLABUS IN DETAIL

In the following pages, suggestions are made for carrying out a four-year syllabus for juniors, indicating the subject-matter, with book-lists and notes on children's activities which are dealt with again in Part III and the Appendices.

Although, in recent years, there has been a swing of opinion away from the traditional class textbook in favour of smaller sets of six or a dozen, as well as single copies, of various informative books, many teachers continue to use one main textbook, as an 'anchor book', while making available as many additional sources of information as possible. One hopes that increased book allowances will permit this practice to continue. In these pages, the four volumes of *Looking at History* (Black) are taken as the 'anchor book' upon which the syllabus and sequence of teaching are largely based. But, though the books were written expressly for this purpose, the author does not imply that his suggestions for teaching history depend entirely upon any one textbook. However carefully and comprehensively a series of textbooks may be written, it would be very wrong if they conveyed an impression that there was no need to go elsewhere for information. One of the prime aims in teaching history to young children is to encourage them to use books—many books—in their search for facts and knowledge.

THE FIRST JUNIOR YEAR

One obvious criticism of the first year's work is that 'pre-history' occupied an immense tract of time—perhaps half a million years, as far as human beings are concerned, yet the proposal is to study it in about one school term.

Unless care is taken, children will gain the impression that Early Man passed rapidly from his flint tools to bronze and then to iron. In fact, of course, the period during which he used flint implements lasted very much longer than the time in which we have advanced from our first knowledge of iron to the light alloys of modern industry.

However, while it is important never to lose sight of the slow rate at which man made his first material progress, it is not practicable to spend the greater part of the school course on pre-history. Moreover, much of our knowledge of Ancient Man is derived from intelligent guesswork, and our concern is to give children as graphic and lively an understanding of history as lies in our power.

It is suggested that at least one term, or even half the first year, be devoted to what may be called Early Times. Because children of seven and eight years are themselves experiencing growth in new skills more vividly perhaps than at any other stage of their lives, (there is, for instance, no stage more significant than the arrival of reading), they will readily appreciate Early Man's advance from perilous existence along the banks of some primeval river to a somewhat more secure life in the cave. They understand his struggle against the advancing cold of successive Ice Ages, his natural use of sharp stones as implements and weapons, his delight in the discovery of fire and his children's task in keeping it alight, because, in their own short lives, they have known experiences and discoveries which were not dissimilar.

Without troubling eight-year-olds with such terms as Paleolithic and Megalithic, we shall show them the advancing skills of the hunters and herdsmen of the Stone Ages to the arrival of bronze in Britain (about 2,000 B.C.), and the comparatively swift advance in living which accompanied the use of metals.

STORIES OF EARLY MAN

If it is agreed that history should be taught to juniors through the social life of people and through stories of men and women, there may be the difficulty that these earliest times have left no stories of individual people. On the other hand, the progress and vicissitudes of Cave Man make up a coherent and fascinating story, and it is not difficult to invent a family called Wolf or Ug in order to present a vivid account of life in the Stone Age. Children delight in hearing how Ug went hunting while his wife stayed at home to scrape skins and the children tended the fire or searched for berries to eat and flints to be chipped. They will learn how the family repelled wild animals and enemies seeking to oust them from their cave, and how they themselves were forced to move to fresh hunting grounds which led them to erect shelters of boughs and skins.

For those who doubt their inventive powers, there are a few stories of early people, including a series of little stories called *Children of Other Days* by C. M. Rutley (Arnold), Joyce Reason's *Bran the Bronzesmith* and Lucy Fitch-Perkins's *The Cave Twins*.

FIRST YEAR: FIRST TERM

TEACHING NOTES

Most children are making their first conscious acquaintance with history during their first term in the junior school, and a start which catches their interest and arouses their enthusiasm is valuable. A teacher might begin with a story of how the early boy or girl, living on the banks of a great tropical river, eating berries and small creatures, eked out a perilous existence, or she might begin by telling how the country or town about the school was once covered by vast forest or by the sea. She might prefer to begin simply by producing a flint from her pocket, which would supply her starting point and at once kindle an interest in collecting flints and fossils which abound in some parts of the country. At all events, the class gains a first understanding of life when the mammoth and sabre-toothed tiger roamed Britain.

Not all Stone Age people lived in caves, but cave-life appeals to young children's imaginations. The story of Stone Age Man's advancing skills unfolds itself, without confusing children with the archaeologist's special terms. This is best achieved through a story, either the teacher's own 'Story of Ug and his sister' or those mentioned below, describing how retreating animals caused Cave Man to leave his cave and to make his first attempts at building a house, which advanced from primitive shelters of boughs and skins to pit-dwellings.

The arrival of metals, bronze and iron, leads to an account of a Lake Village; these were less common in Britain than in certain parts of Europe, but the idea of a home on an island makes an immediate appeal to children and much useful history can be learned through this topic. Stonehenge is interesting, especially if children live in southern England, and they may be reminded of primitive peoples in the world today who are at about the same stage of development—pygmies of Central Africa, Aborigines, natives of New Guinea and parts of the Amazon basin.

Children's Activities

Before attempting to start notebooks, a communal wall-sheet might be made on which are pasted children's drawings and cut-outs of prehistoric animals, Early Man, a cave, and flint implements. Another idea is to make a large composite picture, graphically illustrating the work in progress—cut-out caves in a chalk cliff, people in the foreground, cooking and hunting, the forest beyond with its animals, bear-pit, &c.

Whenever illustrative work is done, it should always be accompanied by written captions or selected sentences, however simple, describing the picture.

Class notebooks or smaller 'topic books', called, say, 'My Book of the Stone Age', with decorated covers and pictures, plus short written text; even if this text is only a single sentence, children should be encouraged to compose it themselves and not merely to copy from the board or book, though this may be necessary at first.

Wall-chart or panel called 'Bronze and Iron Ages' with pictures of implements, pots, weapons, plough, Lake Village, &c.

Models: a cave; twig huts; a hill-fort; pit-dwellings—see Appendix I for details.

In suitable areas, collect flints and fossils for the history table; examine possibility of borrowing specimens or loan-case from local museum. Allow children to attempt the difficult task of attaching a wooden handle to a flint to make an axe or spear.

Act: 'Dinner in the Cave' or the return of the hunters to the cave.

Books

Unstead: *Looking at History*, I, pp. 5–23 (Black).
Quennell: *Everyday Life in Prehistoric Times* (Batsford).
Hope and Sankey-Hudson History Books (this famous 'Woolworths' series contains numberless drawings).
Allen: *Living Long Ago* (Johnston and Bacon).
King Penguin: *Prehistoric Animals* (Penguin).
Hume: *The Pilgrim Way*, I (Blackie).
Looking at the Past—Homes (Chatto and Windus).
History through the Ages (O.U.P.).
The Dawn of Civilisation (Thames and Hudson).

Stories

Rutley: *Children of Other Days* (Arnold) Books II–III.
Fitch-Perkins: *The Cave Twins* (Cape).
Stuart: *A Child's Day through the Ages* (Harrap).
Reason: *Bran the Bronzesmith* (Dent).
Kipling: *The Cat that walked by Itself, Just So Stories* (Macmillan).

The History Table

This should be in evidence at every stage in the junior school, to exhibit models, books and collections, flanked by copies of the above books and others, mostly for their pictures, since, with the exception of *Looking at History*, the text is usually too difficult for seven-to-eight-year-olds. The table can be backed or flanked at the sides by one or two pictures, e.g. O.U.P. Wall Pictures, Series II, No. 1. Another obvious arrangement is to use a narrow table, old desk or shelf against the wall to which are fixed narrow shelves of thin batten, 2–2½ in. wide, and on which are placed open copies of books. Similar narrow shelves of strip-wood can be screwed to a backing sheet of thick card, ply or hardboard, which is fixed at the back of a table on which models are set up. Books on the shelves are held in position by elastic or expanding curtain-wires.

FIRST YEAR: SECOND TERM

The Roman Occupation of Britain is a fascinating study for children of any age, and it might be considered a matter for regret that it occurs so early in a child's school-life. However, it is a period which is almost always studied in some detail at the secondary stage, and it may be found more convenient to arrange visits to Roman sites for older juniors.

The wealth of material and of textbooks devoted to the Roman period is so great that a teacher's chief concern will be to simplify and select the information which his eight-year-olds are most likely to retain. Here again, the Quennells are a great standby for any who have not studied the period in detail, but there is a host of reliable books to fortify and revive a teacher's background knowledge.

The story of the Occupation unfolds itself easily. There are, first, Caesar's punitive expeditions and, a hundred years later, the invasion by Claudius' legions of a country already infiltrated by Roman ideas. The stories of Boadicea and Caractacus are dramatic preludes to the peace of Agricola and the urbanization of southern Britain. The people of the towns, of the self-contained villas and of the garrisons in the West and along the Wall will be the subjects of children's models and notebooks. The stories of St. Alban and St. Patrick are sufficiently well authenticated to satisfy the endeavour to tell children only what we believe to be true.

It is probably a mistake to depict the Roman withdrawal as a dramatic event in the year 410, and it would certainly be wrong to confuse young children with an account of the near-collapse of Roman rule (the period of the Count of the Saxon Shore) which was followed by the revival under Diocletian and Constantine.

The 'lost centuries', when Jutish tribes ravaged the country, need present no problem to children who will not find it difficult to understand the destruction by a people who feared and hated Roman ways. But what of King Arthur, who belongs to this time? Should he be disentangled from the romantic legend that invests him with a medieval court? Or was he a half-savage chieftain named Artos the Bear? King Arthur is best left until a later stage; he will certainly appear as a romantic figure in their junior story books.

FIRST YEAR: SECOND TERM

TEACHING NOTES

Begin with oral description of life among the Ancient Britons, but do not stress their savagery (Caesar's account could not have been accurate) since in many parts of Britain, particularly the south and south-west, a well-developed and artistic society existed. See also story of Phidias in *Heroes and Saints* (Black).

Tell the story of Caesar's invasions which were punitive expeditions and not serious attempts at conquest.

During the next century, the infiltration of Roman ideas and trade made the invasion of Claudius' legions an assured success. Resistance centred about the person of Caractacus. (*People in History*, I—Black.)

What sort of people did the Romans seem to the Britons? Children learn about what first impressed them—the soldiers, weapons, fighting-methods and road-building. Towns near the sites of British settlements—Verulamium, Camulodonum—consult Ordnance Survey Map of Roman Britain and local museum to ascertain position of Roman sites near school.

Mal-administration by officials caused the revolt of Boadicea (see *People in History*, I) which was followed by Agricola's urbanization of southern Britain.

At this stage, build up a picture of life in Roman Britain—the town—the villa (which was a country house and estate as distinct from the town-house)—domestic life, amusements (chariot-races, gladiators, theatre), fortresses on Welsh border and Hadrian's Wall.

More stories: St. Alban, the first martyr in Britain; St. Patrick. (*People in History*, I); Emperor Hadrian (*Heroes and Saints*).

Children's Activities

Notebooks and/or wall-panels will depict Roman galley, soldiers, weapons, domestic heating, mosaic floor, arch, aqueduct.

Describe the street scene on p. 37, *Looking at History*, I.

Make up a group 'strip' of pictures illustrating the story of Alban or Patrick (further suggestions for written work in Appendix I).

Acting: The capture of Caer Caradoc; Caractacus before the Emperor; the humiliation of Boadicea; dinner in a Roman house.

Models: Roman villa or shop; Hypocaust (see Appendix II); a model (or wall-panel) of a Roman town is not impossible (see plan in Quennell, or, simpler, in Ginn's *Roman Towns and Country Houses*).

Books

    Unstead: *Looking at History*, I; *Heroes and Saints*; *People in History*, I.
    Quennell: *Everyday Life in Roman Britain* (Batsford).
    Taylor: *A Soldier on Hadrian's Wall* (O.U.P.).
    History Through the Ages (O.U.P.).
    Titterton: *Roman Soldiers, Roman Towns* (Ginn).
    White: *A Romano-British Family* (O.U.P.).

FIRST YEAR: THIRD TERM

Children learning about the homes and customs of the Saxon invaders come next to the story of St. Augustine and the re-establishment of Christianity, which leads on to the more eventful stories of St. Columba, St. Aidan and the Abbess Hilda. These will not only satisfy a love of stories which are 'true', but may convince children that heroism and courage are not confined to those who kill their fellow-beings.

What other stories might be told to children at this stage? Bede and Caedmon, certainly; Ethelred, perhaps, and Canute, if one cares for the tale of his rebuke to his flatterers. But it is well to remember that too many stories, especially where their substance is thin, can degenerate into mere anecdotage. In history, as in most subjects, there is always the temptation to talk too much and to teach too much too quickly. Moreover, there are a great many activities that eight-year-olds are bursting to carry out themselves.

If children are to retain any clear impression at all, they need at this stage, strong, clear outlines. Therefore, it is probably wise to restrict stories of actual people to no more than twelve during this first year. This may be found to be about the right number of biographies for each junior year. There is then time to make each figure memorable through the presentation, through drawings and dramatization. The effect of too many anecdotes about insignificant kings can be this:

'Soon after this event Egg-Kings were found on the thrones of all these kingdoms, such as Eggberd, Eggbreth, Eggfroth, &c. None of them however succeeded in becoming memorable— except so far as it is difficult to forget such names as Eggbirth, Eggbred, Eggbeard, Eggfilth, &c. Nor is it even remembered by what kind of Eggdeath they perished.' (from *1066 And All That*).

But there is still one great figure who should round off the first year's work, the only monarch in our history who has ever been known as 'the Great'—Alfred, King of Wessex. He must be presented to children as *the* hero-king of all time. (It is worth noting that in Arthur Bryant's *The Story of England: Makers of the Realm*, one of its twelve long chapters is simply titled 'Alfred'.) There is, fortunately, a wealth of stories about him, without having recourse to the tale of the burnt cakes.

FIRST YEAR: THIRD TERM

TEACHING NOTES

Use atlases and blackboard to show children where Angles and Saxons came from, how they crossed the North Sea, raided the coasts, sailing up the rivers and gradually settled in the country, driving the native Britons westwards; children can find places ending with -ham and -ton, and, later in the term, Danish endings, -thorpe, -ness, -by.

Ships and Sailing (Ginn); *Everyday Life in Anglo Saxon, Viking and Norman Times* (Batsford); Saxon homes *How people lived* (O.U.P.); *Homes of Angles and Saxons* (Ginn); *The First Book of the Vikings* (Ward).

Stories of the survival and re-emergence of Christianity are to be found in *People in History*, I (Black)—St. Augustine, St. Columba, St. Aidan, Hilda and Caedmon in *Heroes and Saints*—Ethelburga, St. Cuthbert, Bede. For stories of Norse gods see *Children's Bookshelf* (Harrap).

The coming of the Danes is best described through stories of King Alfred (see *People in History*, I, and Arnold's '*A.L.*' *Readers* series).

Children's activities

A large pictorial map showing Saxon cut-out ships coming across North

Sea to east coast, with pictures of ruined Roman villa, Saxon dwellings.

Illustrated notebooks (e.g. 'My Book about the Angles and Saxons') with ships, weapons, brooches, Saxon homestead, early church.

Attempt a copy of an illuminated manuscript with its capital letter (coloured postcard reproductions from British Museum).

Suggestions for written work in First-Year Notebooks—see Appendix I.

Acting: Caedmon, Paulinus and the King, Alcuin and Charlemagne, Alfred in the Danes' camp.

Models: A Saxon hall (Appendix II); Viking long-ship (Ginn, *Ships and Sailing*; *The Story of Ships*, Methuen).

Books

 Heroes and Saints (Black).
 Looking at History, I (Black).
 People in History, I (Black).
 A Child's Day through the Ages (Harrap).
 How People Lived (O.U.P.—Wall Pictures, Series I, Nos. 2 and 3 are particularly useful).
 Quennell: *Everyday Life in Anglo-Saxon, Viking and Norman Times* (Batsford).
 The Pilgrim Way, I (Blackie).
 Looking at the Past—Homes (Chatto and Windus).
 The First Book of the Vikings (Ward).
 Boucher: *A Viking Raider* (O.U.P.).
 Grice: *A Northumbrian Missionary* (O.U.P.).
 Sutcliff: *A Saxon Settler* (O.U.P.).

STORIES

At this point, it may be appropriate to consider the importance of stories throughout the whole junior course. Of them, the Ministry of Education Pamphlet, No. 23, *Teaching History* says,

'By magic too, the magic of a well-told story, most good teachers have tried to introduce their pupils, if not to history, at least to the stuff of history, if not to the panorama, at least to the tableau, if not to the period, at least to the "timeless moment". If history in its full sense explains and interprets heritage, these stories are among the most precious parts of that heritage itself. They are at the root of an interest in history and their inspiration sends the archaeologist to his "dig", the historian to his research. Well chosen and well told they are self-justified. They stimulate the child's imagination and extend his experience.'

The actual selection of stories is largely a matter of personal preference, though there must be some which can hardly be omitted, for it must never be forgotten that the old stories which are told year in and year out by teachers are unfolding for the first time to their spellbound listeners.

The best source of stories which are biographical is still the *Dictionary of National Biography*. Though it is the source from which most children's writers draw their material, it is well worth while for teachers to consult it themselves and to frame their own versions from its pages.

For children, there is no better way of learning than to listen to their teacher telling a good story. Telling is so much better than reading it, that it is worth the effort of looking up a story and committing its outlines to memory, glancing at one's notes or textbook for those words uttered at the time, which have the authentic flavour of actuality which we cannot hope to surpass. There is, for instance, Becket's reply to the four knights down the darkened cathedral,

'Lo, I am here, no traitor, but a priest of God.'

Or sometimes there are the words written at the time by a chronicler or reporter—for instance, the superb little passage from the *Manchester Guardian*, written in 1910 at the funeral of Florence Nightingale, and quoted in Pamphlet No. 23—

'As the body was borne into the church there was sitting in the porch a little old man in decent black, wearing pinned on his waistcoat the Crimea medal with the Sebastopol clasp. Once he was Private Kneller of the 23rd Foot, now old Mr. Kneller, the Crimean veteran of Romsey. If you talked to this cheerful veteran he would readily tell you how in the trenches before Sebastopol he was shot in the eye and was taken to hospital at Scutari—how as he lay in the ward there night by night he would see a tall lady going along past the beds carrying a lamp. He does not remember at all whether she ever spoke to him, nor whether he spoke to her but he remembers like a spark in the embers of his dwindling mind the apparition of the lady who came softly along the beds at night carrying in her hand a lantern—"one of them old-fashioned lanterns".'

And there was at least one writer equally skilled eight hundred years earlier:

> He caused castles to be built
> which were a sore burden to the poor.
> A hard man was the king
> And took from his subjects many marks
> In gold and many more hundreds of pounds in silver.
> He was sunk in greed
> And utterly given up to avarice.
> He set apart a vast deer preserve and imposed laws concerning it.
> Whoever slew a hart or hind was to be blinded.
> He forbade the killing of boars
> Even as the killing of harts.
> For he loved the stags as dearly
> As though he had been their father . . .
> May Almighty God show mercy to his soul
> And pardon him his sins.
>
> (Anglo-Saxon Chronicle.)

All real learning has to be active, and story-telling by the teacher should arouse mental activity on the part of the children as much as if they were writing or modelling. Listening can be a passive, sluggish occupation, or it can be an intensely active mental process. A teacher who begins a lesson with, 'I am going to tell you about the Pilgrim Fathers', cannot expect the same rustle of interest as if she commenced with 'Suppose you landed on the shore of a land where Red Indians lived, how would you start building your new home?'

For those who cannot consult the *Dictionary of National Biography* there is a great deal of good biography upon the shelves of any library, and there ought to be some in the library or staff-room of every junior school. Suitable books would include a copy of *Oxford Junior Encyclopaedia*, Vol. V, 'Great Lives', as well as Stuart's *A Child's Day Through the Ages*, Power's *Boys and Girls of History* and *Mediaeval People*, Marshall's *Our Island Story* and *Scotland's Story*. Other useful titles are *A Book of Discovery* (Synge), *History Through Great Lives* (Cassell), O.U.P.'s *Living Names* and *Lives of Great Men and Women*, *Who's Who in History* (Blackwell), *Lives to Remember* (Black), *100 Great Lives* (Odhams) and Collins *Brief Lives* series.

Among school textbooks, there are several collections of short biographical stories of nearly all the characters likely to appeal to junior children. But these are rarely arranged in chronological periods and must usually be sought in any one of a set of four books, with a consequent variation in tone and standard of vocabulary difficulty. *People in History*, however, was written for the syllabus described in this book, so that each of its four books is a companion to *Looking at History*. The four books of *Men and Women in History* (Black) contain more stories of people in each period.

But from whatever source stories are drawn, teachers should make every effort to present them unadorned with sickly romanticizing or legendary half-truths. There is an abundance of good material without having to perpetuate such apocryphal tales as Raleigh's cloak, Alfred's cakes, the game of bowls, Bruce's spider, Watt and his kettle or even the murder of the princes in the Tower. As Catherine Firth says,

'The difficulty lies, often, less in the accessibility of information than in the curiously common idea that so long as children are "interested", the accuracy of what they are told is of little importance. But history is a true story. It has no meaning otherwise. To present a child with "fancy" pictures, with untruly coloured incidents, with rhetorical rhapsodizings, with generalizations apart from evidence, or statements slovenly and confused, is to make the learning of history impossible for him and to give him something of much less value than a fairy tale. Remove history from the region of the actual and you leave it hanging between two worlds, a bridge which rests on neither bank, a place where no sure foothold may be gained. The teacher of history who does not "mind" about historical accuracy had far better leave the child alone and let him pursue without hindrance his own desire to find out what happened.'

Of course, history is a great deal more than a series of unrelated, enjoyable stories. That is why this simple scheme for the junior school advocates that each year shall be devoted to a broad period of history which is in many ways a unity, however loose. Then the stories about particular people will arise from a background about which children are gaining an increasing understanding.

THE SECOND JUNIOR YEAR

The nine-year-olds, of what was formerly called Standard Two, will begin or, rather, will carry on from the Normans and may spend the whole year entranced by the Middle Ages.

It is a vast and crowded canvas which will test the teacher's powers of selection and of self-denial in the matter of chalk and talk. It begins, then, with Harold's doomed reign that ended under the great yellow banner of Wessex on Senlac Hill, or, as the Anglo-Saxon Chronicle says, 'at the grey apple tree'. The children learn how William imposed the rule of his Norman followers with castles and his own conception of kingship, while, at the other end of Britain, Saint Margaret, Queen of Scotland, was introducing gentler manners to that northern kingdom.

As has already been said, it is important to avoid presenting medieval people as rather simpler versions of ourselves. There is a very natural tendency to look upon the remote past as upon our childhood—a time when life was much less complicated, when minds and imaginations were still unformed and when actions and emotions were violently expressed.

This is of course very far from the truth. King John, for instance, was much more than a self-willed glutton; he was a highly talented, if wicked, man with an extraordinary understanding of how to manœuvre the intricacies of medieval law and custom to his own advantage. The men who juggled with doctrinal points, who built

Wells Cathedral and Dover Castle, who interpreted the laws of inheritance and land tenure, were men of formidable intellectual calibre.

To some extent, however, children can feel a more personal understanding of these remote days than of, say, the Victorian era. They understand men who allied beauty with usefulness, fashioning their waterspouts into gargoyles which also frightened off evil spirits, and making their superb carvings, not only for the glory of God, but also to teach the Bible stories to an illiterate people. They can understand the fervour and love of fighting which drove men to the Crusades and the French Wars, from which, if they survived, they brought home carpets, glass and new ideas. Children's acute sense of what is 'fair' appreciates the justice of dividing arable land into half-acre strips and of punishing wrong-doers by holding them to public ridicule. But it is wrong always to make them feel indignant for the poor peasant who had to carry out 'week work' for the lord, since that was an arrangement which was for a long time to the advantage of both parties.

The story of how people—the monks, peasants, merchants and apprentices, the knights, bowmen, wandering players and outlaws— lived in the Middle Ages is full of rich and vivid detail for nine-year-olds. There is a great deal to do, act, draw and hear about, perhaps too much, so the stories of people who lived in these tumultuous times must be carefully chosen and skilfully told.

If any understanding of the Middle Ages in Britain is to be achieved, we cannot leave out the stories of William I, Becket, and Richard Cœur de Lion, for they personify strong kingship, the Church and the Crusader, all dominant ideas in men's minds. The great patriots who resisted Edward I, Llewellyn, Wallace and Bruce, must also have their place. There is compassion in the story of Queen Philippa at Calais, medieval warfare at Agincourt, the anger of the peasants in Wat Tyler's story and the growth of learning and literature in the lives of Chaucer and Caxton. Moreover, all are dramatic, thrilling stories.

Magna Carta, de Montfort's Parliament and the involved contests between kings and barons are topics which may be left alone in the junior school. It is doubtful if they can create anything but confusion in the mind of a child of nine or ten years. If we wish to show children the uncertainty and lawlessness that existed during the barons' wars when the country lacked a strong ruler, we can tell them how Margaret Paston was besieged at Gresham by a neighbour's force of a thousand men, who dragged her from her own house and sacked it in front of her eyes. Her husband wrote to the King about it,

'The 28th day of January last past, the said Lord sent to the said mansion a riotous people to the number of a thousand persons . . . arrayed in manner of war, with cuirasses, coats of mail, steel helmets, glaives, bows, arrows, large shields, guns, pans of fire, long cromes to draw down houses, ladders and picks with which they mined down the walls, and long trees with which they broke up gates and doors, and so came into the said mansion, the wife of your beseecher at that time being therein, and twelve persons with her—the which persons they drove out of the said mansion, and mined down the walls of the chamber wherein the wife of your said beseecher was, and bare her out at the gates and cut asunder the posts of the houses and let them fall, and broke up all the chambers and coffers in the said mansion, and rifled . . . and bare away stuff, array and money . . . to the value of £200.' (See *The Pastons and their England* and, for children, *Princes and Rebels*.)

SECOND YEAR

TEACHING NOTES

To avoid the dangers of a diffuse, vague impression of so complicated a period as the Middle Ages, teachers may feel that their work will have more point if they concentrate upon particular places of interest, especially if their school happens to be in an ancient town or city. Thus, the year's work would be concerned with

(i) a medieval village, imaginary or particular, in, say, the fourteenth or fifteenth centuries, with emphasis upon the people in it, their names, work, amusements and troubles.

(ii) From this starting-point, interest will clearly go outside the village and its surrounding forest to the Castle and the Monastery.

(Here it is well to remember the dangers of confusing children by emphasizing the exceptions, complications and embellishments of any historical institution; castles and monasteries underwent many changes and modifications during the centuries when they had vigorous life; a simplified version of each which is broadly true and characteristic must be chosen, such as may be found in *Looking at History*, II.*)

(iii) Beyond the village and monastery lies the Medieval Town, which can provide at least a term's study, with its streets, gilds, trades, amusements and organized social life (see Ch. 20, *The Medieval Scene* (Black)).

Ample material for the approach outlined above will be found in the lists and activities suggested later, but many teachers may prefer the following scheme based on *Looking at History* Book II, with its companion *People in History*, II—*William I to Caxton*. Additional stories for the period are to be found in *Princes and Rebels*.

FIRST TERM:

The Norman Invasion—tell the story of William I (*People in History*, II) —for adults, there is a brilliant version of the battle in Bryher's *The Fourteenth of October*, excerpts from which will appeal to children.

Children study parts of *The Bayeux Tapestry* (Penguin book) which may suggest to them an effective way of recording their own knowledge of the Normans.

Continue with how William built castles and ordered the Domesday Book to be compiled.

A story—Good Queen Margaret of Scotland.

Village life—children act the ceremony of homage, punishments (the bad baker, &c.), trial by ordeal.

Two stories—Henry II and Becket Hugh of Lincoln.

Children's Activities

A frieze version of the Bayeux Tapestry showing the invasion and battle.

Plan of a village, showing the two- or three-field system, church, mill, cotts, castle, forest.

Notebooks: Norman armour and clothes; the castle, its main sections; or topic booklets, e.g., 'A Norman Castle', 'Work On the Manor', 'Punishments'.

* Attention is drawn to two errors in some copies of *Looking at History*—on pp. 10, 11, the entrance to the keep of a Norman castle was normally up a flight of steps, and on p. 19 for 'villeins (or serfs)' read 'villeins (or peasants)'—a serf was a landless man with no rights comparable to those of a villein.

Acting: the ceremony of homage; the Manor Court; punishments; ordeal by fire, by combat.

Models (see Appendix II): Norman castle; Manorial village; a Norman hall; stocks, pillory.

Note: a variation of the usual Norman castle can be made in stiffish card which is fixed by bent flaps at eye level to a display board, with the base of two corner towers resting on table or shelf, each floor of the castle is attached to wall-board, so that the children build up a section through the keep of a castle (as shown on p. 11, *Looking at History*, II).

Books: see end of this section.

SECOND TERM

The monastery: its functions, main parts and officers.

How men fought—weapons and armour—stories of Richard I, Llewelyn, Bruce, Queen Philippa, the Black Prince, Owen Glendower.

Travellers, pilgrims, scholars—Chaucer and the Canterbury Pilgrims, Roger Bacon.

Children's Activities

Wall-chart—a plan of a monastery (this is a difficult model for nine-year-olds, though it certainly can be attempted; in some cases a wall-chart may be preferable).

Notebooks: Brother Hugh's day; Crusaders' shields, ship, siege tower; written work—see Appendix I.

Acting: Richard I and his page—how Richard was captured; Bruce and the gift of spurs; Bruce and Comyn; Queen Philippa and the burghers of Calais; Hugh and Henry II in the forest; Glendower's escape.

Models: see Appendix II.

THIRD TERM

The medieval town—the streets and houses; the tournament; clothes; amusements; food; poor people; learning.

Stories: Wat Tyler; Henry V; William Caxton; James I of Scotland.

Children's Activities

For written work—see Appendix I.

Notebooks or topic booklets—some general notes, but since children in at least the 'A' stream will be beginning to want to ferret out information for themselves, encourage them to choose one or two topics from a list, as above, in order to write and illustrate a little booklet about each, e.g. 'My Book About Food In the Middle Ages'; 'My House in Mercery Lane'.

Acting: a medieval street scene, apprentices bawling their wares, water-carrier, shoppers, merchants, the mayor, town constable, beggars, lepers —each child says who he is and what he does.

Wat Tyler—kills the tax-collector, raises the peasants, releases John Ball, marches to London, &c.

The King visits Caxton: Catherine Douglas tries to save the King.

(This is the most vigorous and unselfconscious stage for acting; some-times one can suggest two or three subjects similar to those above each to be worked out by a small group and performed one after another in a few days' time—miming will often get this activity under way.)

Model: a medieval town—see Appendix II.

BOOKS
(The inexperienced teacher who is momentarily daunted by all the suggestions above may take comfort in the thought that it is unlikely that more than a selection of these topics and activities would be at-tempted).

Unstead: *The Middle Ages* (*Looking at History,* Book II); *William I to Caxton* (*People in History,* Book II); *The Medieval Scene; Monasteries; Princes and Rebels* (Black).

Reeves: *The Medieval Town, The Medieval Village* (Longmans).

Haden Guest: *Your Hearth and Home* (Allen and Unwin).

History Bookshelves—Green Shelf (Ginn).

The Bayeux Tapestry (Penguin).

Pearce (ed.): *People of the Past,* series C (O.U.P.).

Rockcliff New Project Series—*The Middle Ages* (Rockcliff).

Stuart: *A Child's Day Through the Ages* (Harrap).

Power: *Boys and Girls of History* (O.U.P.).

Sellman: *Castles and Fortresses* (Methuen).

Wilkinson: *Arms and Armour* (Black).

Quennell: *A History of Everyday Things in England;* I (Batsford).

Harrison: *The Middle Ages* (Hulton).

Oakeshott: *A Knight and His Weapons* (Lutterworth).

THE THIRD JUNIOR YEAR

Ten-year-olds, full of zest for adventure, for exploring, and for tales of treasure and violence, devour the period of the Tudor and Stuart monarchs.

It is a tremendous period of history, in every sense, and, again, the teacher will be hard put to make a selection which will preserve some feeling and understanding of these two centuries during which England underwent so many changes in her social, religious and political life.

The themes and topics include the Reformation, the struggle with Spain, the expansion of trade and learning, the voyages of discovery, the work, amusements and social distress of Elizabeth's reign; there are, too, Guy Fawkes, the Pilgrim Fathers, the Civil War, Cromwell, the remarkable reign of Charles II, William and Mary, Marlborough and Anne.

As always, it is essential to consider these topics through the eyes of a child and through our knowledge of his interests and characteristics. Not for him are the causes in detail of enmity with Spain or of the triumph of Parliament over the King, nor the tortuous diplomacy of Charles II or Marlborough. But he will be stirred by the colour, action and romance of Tudor and Stuart times.

The despotism of Henry VIII and something of the nature of the Reformation is best conveyed to children through the stories of Wolsey and Thomas More; let them hear More's own words on the scaffold,

'I pray thee help me safely up, but for my coming down, let me shift for myself',

and his last words, that echo all the martyrs of the time,

'I die, the King's loyal servant, but God's servant first.'

The struggle with Spain is told through Drake's apprenticeship at San Juan, his revenge at Nombre de Dios, his voyage round the world and, of course, the Armada. Raleigh's story illustrates the tricky course of the courtier and early colonizer. Chancellor and Fitch are the intrepid, almost unsung, Merchant Adventurers, while the tale of Will Shakespeare, as far as we know it, calls up the life of Tudor London, its rowdy apprentices, players, watermen, beggars and rogues, as well as the plays at the 'Curtain' and 'Globe'.

Dover Wilson's *Life in Shakespeare's England* is a mine of fascinating information from contemporary writing, some of which will appeal to children:

'These hookers, or anglers, be perilous and most wicked knaves. They commonly go in frieze jerkins and galy-slops pointed beneath the knee. These when they practise their pilfering, it is all by night; for, as they walk a-day-times from house to house, to demand charity, they vigilantly mark where or in what place they may attain to their prey, casting their eyes up to every window, well noting what they see there, whether apparel or linen, hanging near the said windows, and that they will be sure to have the next night following. For they customably carry with them a staff of five or six foot long, in which, within one inch of the top thereof, is a little hole bored through, in which hole they put an iron hook, and with the same they will pluck unto them anything that they may reach therewith, which hook in the daytime they covertly carry about with them. . . .

I was credibly informed that a hooker came to a farmer's house in the dead of night, and putting back a draw-window of a low chamber, the bed standing hard by the same window, in which lay three persons (a man and two big boys), this hooker with his staff plucked off their garments which lay upon them to keep them warm, with the coverlet and sheet, and left them lying asleep naked save their shirts, and had away all clean, and never could understand where it became. I verily suppose that when they were well waked with cold, they surely thought that Robin Goodfellow (according to the old saying) had been with them that night.'

The story of the *Mayflower* Pilgrims is a wonderful tale of how they suffered on the voyage out, built their settlement at Thievish Harbour, re-named New Plymouth, and lost fully half their tiny company during the first terrible winter, so that Captain Standish levelled the graves on Fort Hill to prevent the prowling Indians from reckoning up the few that remained alive.

The Civil War is a difficult episode to teach to children; its causes, course and results are very involved, and, even at this long distance, prejudice and bias are by no means dead. To present it as a simple conflict between dashing Cavaliers and sombre Roundheads is so risky that many teachers will prefer merely to describe with the help of contemporary sources some of the main happenings.

For the Plague and the Great Fire, our report is reinforced by that lively eye-witness, Sam Pepys, and, to conclude the stories of this period, there would be John and Sarah Churchill, not forgetting how Sarah engineered Anne's escape from her ruined father, James II, down the back stairs, losing a royal shoe in the muddy street before they reached the safety of a coach and an armed bishop's house!

Around these stories, perhaps a dozen or so, can be built the background of splendour and wretchedness that is vital to a first understanding of the period. An immense amount of material and a great many people must be omitted in order to retain some clarity in the mind of a child. It is impossible to resist one more example of the confusion that alone remains from a syllabus overcrowded and unsuited to young children:

'One of the most romantic aspects of the Elizabethan age was the wave of beards which suddenly swept across history and settled upon the great men of the period. The most memorable of these beards was the cause of the outstanding event of the reign, which occurred in the following way.

THE GREAT ARMADILLO

The Spaniards complained that Captain F. Drake, the memorable bowlsman, had singed the King of Spain's beard (or Spanish Mane, as it was called) one day when it was in Cadiz Harbour. Drake replied that he was in his hammock at the time and a thousand miles away. The King of Spain however insisted that the beard had been spoilt and sent the Great Spanish Armadillo to ravish the shores of England.

The crisis was boldly faced in England, especially by Big Bess herself, who instantly put on an enormous quantity of clothing and rode to and fro on a white horse at Tilbury. . . .' (from *1066 And All That*).

THIRD YEAR

TEACHING NOTES

Many teachers will choose to spend at least two of the three terms of this year with the Tudors, and chiefly the Elizabethan era, leaving the remainder of the time to the Stuarts.

THE TUDORS

Ten-year-olds begin to have some time-sense and it may be well to open the Tudor period with the story of Sir Thomas More (apart from a passing reference, it is wasting time to dwell upon Henry VIII's marital adventures, and it is doubtful if room can be found at this stage for Lady Jane Grey's pathetic story).

Having thus launched the period, find out (and the emphasis in these third and fourth years is upon 'finding out') with the children about

1. Tudor homes, furniture and clothes;
2. Tudor ships and seamen;
3. The Great Queen;
4. Amusements—principally the 'Globe', but also bear-baiting, dancing, smoking, travel.

These four lines of approach alone will suggest 'booklets' which children can now compile with skill as well as enthusiasm, not forgetting the use of cut-outs and postcards as well as drawings and tracings.

Ships and Seamen of this era can be a study in itself; stories of Chancellor, Francis Drake and the Armada must be included, while 'The Revenge' and 'Admirals All' in English lessons will introduce other sea-dogs, such as Hawkins, Grenville, Frobisher and Gilbert.

For further reading, stories of the Cabots, Lady Jane Grey, Hawkins, Sir Philip Sidney, John Smith, Wm. Harvey, Rupert, Dampier and Celia Fiennes are to be found in *Discoverers and Adventurers* (Black).

Children's Work on the Tudors

For suggestions for written work, see Appendix I and for modelling, Appendix II; children at this stage are often adept at dressing figures and puppets, especially as the costumes of this period are attractive to make and draw.

The following are suggestions for titles to booklets of say, 4–12 pages—
'Tudor Ships', 'Tudor Sailors', 'A Tudor House', 'Tudor Furniture',
'Tudor Clothes', 'Elizabethan Children', 'At the Globe', 'Games and
Pastimes'.

Acting: for a Christmas play, the medieval *St. George and the Dragon*
play is an excellent example of the rollicking entertainment that was
popular at this time.

A. A. Milne's *The Woodcutter and The Princess* can be given a Tudor
setting.

THE STUARTS

A selection has to be made from a crowded period; there can be reference to the Gunpowder Plot, while the story of Raleigh helps to indicate
the character of James I as well as the hero's.

In *People in History*, III is a story of one of the women who sailed in
he *Mayflower*, since the determination and dogged will of the Puritan sects
is an important aspect of this period.

It will be wise to avoid the causes and course of the Civil War and
sufficient to mention Rupert and the Cavaliers, as well as Cromwell and
the Ironsides, though it will be difficult to avoid a romantic tenderness for
the former! It is a matter of opinion whether the character and achievements of Cromwell should be considered by juniors; the author of this
book feels that they are beyond most eleven-year-olds. The story of
Montrose provides a stirring tale of the Civil War and should remind
English children of the importance of Scotland in our national history.

Stuart London is a rewarding study, because of the amount of available
material and because its relative importance was even greater than today.
The stories of the Plague and the Great Fire are best described through
the story of Pepys and with the use of suitable passages from the Diary.

A topic: Travel in Stuart times.

Stories: John and Sarah Churchill; the Escape of Lord Nithsdale (this
actually occurred after the '15 Rebellion and, strictly, is just outside the
reign of the last Stuart monarch). The exploits of Captain Smith and
Dampier are exciting and important while William Harvey is a major
figure of history.

Children's Work on the Stuarts

This should continue along the lines indicated for the Tudor period
and as suggested in Appendices I and II. Children record their findings in
their notebooks, topic booklets, with dressed figures, and on wall-friezes

and panels; titles for booklets might include: 'The Gunpowder Plot'; 'Dinner With Mr. Pepys'; 'The Great Fire told by Will Hewer, servant to Mr. Pepys'; 'Travel in Stuart Times'; 'Stuart London'; 'My New House in Bread Street'; 'A Stuart Doctor'; 'Among the Red Indians'; 'A Pirate's Story'.

BOOKS

Unstead: *Tudors and Stuarts* (*Looking at History*, III); *People in History*, III; *A History of Houses*; *Travel by Road*; *Discoverers and Adventurers* (Black).

Firth: *Under Tudor Rulers* (Ginn: Yellow Shelf).

Quennell: *A History of Everyday Things*, Vol. 2 (Batsford).

Allen: *The Story of Your Home* (Faber).

Allen: *Stuart England* (Rockcliff).

Pearce (ed.): *People of the Past*, series D & E (O.U.P.).

Reeves: *Elizabethan Court, Elizabethan Citizen* (Longmans).

Robinson: *Elizabethan Ship* (Longmans).

Synge: *A Book of Discovery* (Nelson).

Schroeder: *Looking at the Past* (Chatto and Windus).

Hoare: *Travel by Sea* (Black).

Male: *The Story of the Theatre* (Black).

'Jackdaw' series: No. 2, *The Plague and The Fire of London*; No. 5, *The Armada*; No. 6, *The Gunpowder Plot* (Cape).

THE FOURTH JUNIOR YEAR

It is a fairly common practice in many schools to adopt a similar syllabus to the one that has been outlined, but to take it at a rather slower pace. Thus, the first year may be devoted to ancient civilizations, the second to pre-Conquest British history, the third to the Middle Ages and the fourth to the Tudors and Stuarts. It is felt that this scheme has greater thoroughness, and that it also takes advantage of the junior's love of the colour and romance which are traditionally associated with the remoter past; also, he is thought to be too young to be concerned with the involved course of modern history and with such protracted movements as the Napoleonic Wars and the Industrial Revolution.

There is certainly a good deal to be said for this point of view, but it nevertheless seems a pity that eleven-year-old children with lively and inquiring minds should not be given the opportunity for acquaintance with some of the outstanding happenings and people of the last 250 years, especially when one reflects that most of them, in their secondary schools, will return to a study of the Ancient World and will not 'reach' modern history for several years.

It must be possible to select a number of historical topics from the last two and a half centuries, without losing sight of the main concern in teaching history to juniors—the story of people and how they lived. Here, then, are some suggestions for a fourth-year junior course.

Stories can include some of the adventures of Bonnie Prince Charlie (at least until he left these shores!). Wolfe, Clive, John Wesley and Fry make strong claims for inclusion, with the inventors Watt and Stephenson and the national heroes, Nelson and Wellington. In the eighteenth century, Georgian homes, reformers, ships, coaches, town and country work, games and pastimes are topics within the grasp of ten year-olds.

In the nineteenth century, topics would include railways and steamships, Shaftesbury's work for children, Florence Nightingale, Robert Owen and Livingstone.

Lastly, in the twentieth century, one might choose to look at the development of inventions which have affected our everyday lives —wireless, motor-cars, aeroplanes and television.

The task of selection and omission in this fourth year is perhaps more difficult because of the voluminous mass of information which exists about modern people and events. It may, therefore, be worth mentioning some topics which have no place in the junior school. At this stage, the importance of Walpole, the causes and course of the eighteenth-century struggle with France, and the loss of the American colonies are best disregarded. The achievements of statesmen such as the two Pitts, Gladstone, Palmerston and Disraeli cannot possibly appeal to young children. While it may seem illogical to include the story of Nelson and to omit the career of Napoleon, a moment's thought on the capabilities of juniors will justify leaving the French Revolution and Bonaparte to the secondary stage. The Industrial Revolution is gloomy stuff for juniors except when one deals with Shaftesbury and the children, and it is extremely doubtful if there is value in describing any inventions other than Watt's and Stephenson's improvements.

The causes, courses and results of wars are always to be avoided, because—it seems superfluous to repeat—young children are interested in people and not in abstractions. It is difficult to find heroes of any lasting stature in modern global warfare, but some teachers may feel that the achievements of T. E. Lawrence in the First World War, and of Sir Winston Churchill in the Second, quite different in scale though they be, can be made intelligible to children.

FOURTH YEAR
TEACHING NOTES

First Term

Georgian England: commence with the story of Bonnie Prince Charlie. Develop as topics: *How people travelled—*
- (i) *The Coaching Age*—highwaymen—inns—roadmakers;
- (ii) *Travel by Sea*—ships—press-gang—smugglers—canals—the story of Captain Cook is appropriate here.

Second line of interest: *How people lived—*
- (i) *Georgian houses*—furniture—gardens—clothes;
- (ii) *Work*—the new farming—beginning of factories (stories: James Watt, Robert Owen);
- (iii) *Soldiers*—uniforms and weapons—stories of Wolfe and Clive (the beginning of Empire);
- (iv) *Play*—sports and amusements—Bath—coffee-houses—early newspapers.

Second Term

The nineteenth century:
- (i) *The Railway Age*—the story of Watt can be taken here rather than in the first term if desired; though Watt died in 1819, his work had an all-important bearing upon the development of nineteenth-century Britain. Follow with the story of George Stephenson.

  The railway mania—town travel—steam ships.

  Stories—Lord Nelson Wellington, Elizabeth Fry.
- (ii) *Queen Victoria's England*—consider two or three aspects which interest children, viz.

43

Poor people—children at work—Lord Shaftesbury, Owen—street life—hawkers—children;

Two women—Florence Nightingale, Elizabeth Garrett Anderson.

Homes—furniture—clothes—the family;

Exploration—David Livingstone.

Third Term

Our century:

Consider a few of the things that children know well and regard as characteristic of this age, and which were hardly suspected in Victoria's time:

Motor cars—early adventures and development;

Aeroplanes;

Wireless and television;

Men of the twentieth century—Scott, Lawrence, Alexander Fleming, Nuffield, Churchill.

Children's Activities

This is the best year for taking juniors out on visits to places of local historical interest—there are few localities without some Georgian houses to draw, or inns that were formerly used in coaching days; schools within reach of London can visit its museums to see examples of eighteenth- and nineteenth-century furniture, machines and vehicles; indeed almost any local museum has something to offer from the last 250 years, if not earlier.

Notebooks should now be at their best with good drawings, tracings and cut-outs. Children might collect information about inns, early vehicles (the London to Brighton run is an annual help for pictures of old cars), aeroplanes, military uniforms, ships, early cricket, Victorian fashions, and railway engines. This variety of topics and the chances of finding enthusiasts in one or more of them makes this an excellent opportunity to encourage individual or joint topic booklets (children often prefer, at this stage, to work in pairs).

Written work, at least in an 'A' stream, should now reach a fairly high standard—suggestions for short booklets: 'Coaches'; 'Highwaymen'; 'Roadmakers'; 'Early Railway Engines'; 'A History of the Bicycle'; 'A Georgian House'; 'Georgian Furniture'; 'Uniforms at Waterloo'; 'A History of Sport'; 'Motor-Cars'; 'My History of Aeroplanes'. In addition there are the subjects for written work suggested in Appendix I.

If preferred, much of the above work can be attractively set out on friezes which can now be termed time-charts, since some eleven-year-olds will be ready to take a chronological view of their history, and there is no reason why a small group should not produce a time-chart of British History illustrating certain aspects—clothes, houses, vehicles, weapons (this can also be done by the whole school, each class contributing cut-outs to friezes which decorate the School Hall—all the pictures required can be found in the four books of *Looking at History*. Many a dull and shabby hall has been enlivened by such friezes, which have also given a boost to the teaching of history through the school).

Models: See suggestions in Appendix II—vehicles are especially popular, but the lines of a Georgian house are so regular that it is easy to cut out doors and windows from thin 'ply', making a street background for the vehicles that is more effective than a painted back-sheet.

A class 'museum' of Victorian objects ranging from 'bun' pennies and stamps to antimacassars and early photographs can be a fascinating exercise: objects must be borrowed and carefully returned.

Books

Unstead: *Queen Anne to Queen Elizabeth II* (*Looking at History*, IV); *People in History*, Book IV; *A History of Houses*; *Travel by Road*; *Great Leaders* (Black).

Quennell: *A History of Everyday Things*, Vols. 3 and 4 (Batsford).

Synge: *A Book of Discovery* (Nelson).

Oxford Junior Encyclopaedia, Vol, 4 (for transport) (O.U.P.).

Ellacott: *Wheels on the Road*, *The Story of Aircraft*, *The Story of Ships* (Methuen).

Power: *Boys and Girls of History* (C.U.P.).

Burke: *Travel in England* (Batsford).

The Changing Shape of Things series (Murray).

Allen: *The Story of Your Home* (Faber).

Elliot: *British History Displayed* (C.U.P.).

Newsom: *A.D. Historical News Sheets* (1 vol. Allen and Unwin).

Hoare: *Travel by Sea*, *The Story of Aircraft* (Black).

Turland: *Furniture in England* (Black).

Allen: *Railways* (Blackwell).

Fry: *Railways* (E.S.A.).

Ransome–Wallis: *British Railways Today* (Black).

'Jackdaw' series: No. 1, *Trafalgar* (Cape).

LOCAL HISTORY

A good deal has been written and said about the value of teaching local history. It is pointed out that children are interested in and proud of their locality, which is therefore a profitable *starting-point*, be it town, village, suburb or New Town.

There is no doubt that a teacher who ignores the district about the school is neglecting what may be a rich source of historical interest, for, even if the opportunities for local studies vary widely, there are few parts of England which are quite bereft of some historical associations. Apart from the help that the public library and museum will give to a teacher who is new to a district, there are always guide books, the Ordnance Survey maps which show pre-Roman, Roman and monastic sites, and books such as *Country Houses open to the Public (Country Life)*. This gives the position, admission days and fees of every important country house in England, one or more of which are usually within reach of a modest class outing.

History exists on every side, in the rounded window of the church, in the road outside the school, in the level-crossing and the inn-sign, but the case to make local history the starting-point for *young* children cannot bear close examination. Young children are usually much less aware of the surroundings which they pass on their way to school than many people have supposed; they are usually far more concerned with their own experiences, their friends and their games.

Their eyes can be opened, and they will be made much more keenly aware of their locality, if their teacher illustrates his lessons with a piece of Roman pottery that was unearthed on the new housing estate, or the fossil that someone found down in the quarry, and if he encourages them to go and see the mound some way off that was once a hillfort, as well as the church with its remaining Norman arch and the list of vicars stretching back to the Armada. Thus, he will be teaching them to look about and 'to see the familiar with fresh eyes'.

At every stage, local history should be used as an illustration, even if this sometimes means doubling back upon the syllabus. If Verul-amium or Caerleon are within reach, the journey may be irksome for first-year juniors, but there is every reason why they should make a half-day trip when they are a little older. Somewhere in the district, there is almost certain to be a house of the Tudor or Stuart period which ten-year-olds should go to see and sketch—if it is Hatfield House, Hampton Court or Little Moreton Hall, Cheshire, they are especially fortunate. Besides Syon House, Castle Howard and Longleat, with its many styles, there are a great many examples of Georgian, Regency and, of course, Victorian architecture for fourth-year children to see in most towns and villages. Some districts are much richer than others, but librarians and museum curators are usually extraordinarily helpful about the treasures in their own area.

Anyone who is engaged in teaching forty children in one class will not minimize the degree of fortitude that is required to organize a visit to the local museum, especially if 'local' means a long walk and two buses to catch! The presence of students in school or a 'floater' on the staff or even a direct request to a head teacher may mean that half a class can be taken at a time but, however it is managed, careful preparation and a preliminary reconnaisance are essential to make a visit to the museum worth while.

The teacher might prepare his class for what they will see, and give them a short list of questions to which they should find the answers, as well as suggesting one or two sketches that they might make. In this way, something will have been done to help children gain more than a jumbled impression of pots behind glass. Molly Harrison's *Learning out of School* (E.S.A.) and Islay Doncaster's *Finding the History Around Us* give useful information about the technique of visiting places of interest.

Many of the livelier museums, of course, lend exhibition cases, and also offer special courses for schools. It is not easy to form and maintain a school museum that has any vitality, though it is sometimes done with great success. Usually, the value of any exhibits is only an immediate one for the children who actually collected the pieces. Sometimes local conditions make it possible to assemble little collections of flints, fossils and Roman tiles; the rusty arrow-head will make its appearance, with a candle-snuffer, a blunderbuss and a piece of a flail. Some of these are then kept for future occasions, but not, one hopes, covered with dust in a glass cupboard in the hall. Top-year classes can occasionally be asked to make an interesting Victorian collection, for it is remarkable what treasures their grand-mothers will lend!

To sum up this outline of a junior history course, one might describe it as a straightforward one that divides British history into four unequal but comprehensible periods, from which the stories of a dozen or so dominant personalities in each are chosen, around whom a picture is built up of the way in which ordinary people lived, worked, travelled and enjoyed themselves. It now remains to consider teaching history in the classroom in rather more detail than has yet been suggested.

PART III

History in the Classroom

FIRST and foremost, the young teacher must plan the year's work. She must think of the period as a whole—it may be Early History or the Middle Ages. She must say to herself, 'Here is a great tract of time in which countless people lived, many of them important; in which a vast number of events occurred, some important from one point of view or another, and all the time people were following a way of life which differed greatly from our own. How am I to give children an understanding of, say, Roman Britain or Medieval England? Which stories shall I tell? Who are the people children will remember? What models, pictures, charts, notebooks shall we make?'

A short time ago, the author overheard two sisters talking as they bent over their wet-evening painting; one said,

'Coo, we had history today!'

Her sister replied, 'Poor you. What was she on about?'

'Oh, Cabots or Gabots or something, I can't remember,'

'She just talks, doesn't she?'

'Well, it wouldn't be so bad if we *did* something—drew pictures or even wrote notes, but we just have to sit and listen!'

This snatch of conversation passed a child's judgement on the earnest lessons of many a conscientious teacher who works hard to teach children about the Tudor seamen or the Norman Invasion. The pity is that, so often, she is the only one in the classroom who is working, and, on the whole, children prefer working to being lectured to.

INFORMATION

A great part of the teaching of history consists of imparting information and facts to children, and the best source of information is still their teacher. But this does not mean that she should invariably lecture for thirty-five minutes and then summarize by ten minutes of questions round the class.

The teacher, one hopes, knows a great deal more about the period of history in question than she will attempt to convey to her children—older children, particularly, will rejoice in the extra snippets of history which she is constantly producing as the term advances and as they are working in their groups—that, for instance, earth floors were hardened with bull's blood or that the urinal was called the 'garde-robe' because clothes were hung up there in the belief that the ammonia fumes protected them from moths, or that boys hardly older than themselves were on board the *Victory* at Trafalgar. Nevertheless, she will select the information for her children having regard to their ages and to what is significant and memorable to them.

When starting a new topic or a fresh period, it is always well to consider its introduction, how to command the children's interest from the outset. With young children, the story approach is almost always the best: 'A long, long, time ago, when there were no houses or fields or roads in our country, but thick forests and grassy hills, a boy named "Strong" lived in a cave. . . .' Similarly, one might open the Norman period with an imaginative account of how a group of ladies wove a great tapestry to tell the story of a battle, or tell with some dramatic force how William heard the news of Harold's accession and straightway vowed to invade England (as in *People in History*, Book II). Sometimes, it is effective to produce from one's pocket a piece of flint, a scrap of Roman tile, an old coin, a book such as *Pilgrim's Progress* or *Pepys's Diary*, and to make that the starting-point of a lesson or topic. In these simple ways, children are not only encouraged to bring along their own treasures and to keep their eyes open, but they more readily appreciate that history is alive and is within their reach.

A good picture is another obvious opening, and it is effective occasionally to read a poem (e.g. Southey's 'After Blenheim') or some arresting passage, for instance this passage from a letter written in the eighteenth century.

'We were now going slowly over a heavy sandy road and the coach rocked a good deal and sometimes stuck, I feared once or twice that we should be overturned, but the squire said "No danger", and to divert my attention, pointed to a gibbet across the heath, on which a highwayman hung in chains, no very pleasant object.

'As I looked towards it, suddenly the open window was blocked up by a horseman with a black crape over his face, crying, "Your money or your lives!" who fired straight through the coach so as to shatter the opposite glass. The next moment another highwayman appeared at the other window. There's no describing the noise, uproar and confusion, the smoke, stench of gunpowder, shrieking of women and barking of the puppy.

'The next moment, our stout old squire, disengaging a blunderbuss from its sling, presented the muzzle full at the highwayman who had not yet fired, and sprang out of the coach with it: on which the man galloped up the bank stooping low so as to keep his horse's neck between his head and the piece.'

A useful source, both of timely information and of spirited presentation of past events as 'hot news', are the 'A.D. Newsheets' (Allen and Unwin); here are the headlines for the sheet which might have appeared in 1666, if the techniques of our modern newspapers had been in vogue at that time—

LONDON SCOURGED BY FIRE

Flames sweep across City: Relief Measures in Hand
Vivid Accounts by Eyewitnesses

There are also the delightful advertisements in the columns of these same news sheets—

'TOBACCO SMOKING. Lessons in Tobacco smoking given to Gentlemen by a former attendant on Sir Walter Raleigh. Strictest privacy. Perfection guaranteed.'

or, again, from the 'issue' of 1642—

'MEN WANTED. Mr. Hampden is raising a regiment of Green Coats. Pay offered: Sgt. 1s. 2d. *per diem*, Drummer 1s. *per diem*, Corporal 10d. *per diem*, Private 8d. *per diem*.'

Having, by story, picture or anecdote, introduced the topic or period to the class, what further sources of information can juniors make use of?

USE OF TEXTBOOKS

This aspect of school work has been sufficiently aired in recent years to make superfluous any discussion about the merits of using separate sets of textbooks as against the old practice of 'reading round the class' from a single set of history books. It is, perhaps, worth remarking that while there is nothing to recommend the latter practice as a regular method, many teachers still prefer to have one full set, or at least half-set, of a reliable 'anchor' textbook for occasional use by the whole class. While they agree that reading-round-the-class is a dull and probably unprofitable way of learning anything, they will often wish to refer all their children to a particular picture or to a passage, which someone will emphasize by reading aloud:

To learn to use a book is an essential part of learning history. Thus, children must be trained to do so; sometimes, they will read a chapter before the lesson, so that the teacher picks up the topic from them. Again, they will often recapitulate by using their books following a lesson. There should be a great deal of reading for information and, one hopes, for pleasure. It is important that reading shall frequently have a specific aim, which is why teachers of older juniors will devise a number of questions to be answered with the aid of the textbook, for instance;

'Read the chapter on Travel and describe a stage-wagon, a post-chaise, a mail-coach. Mention their uses, cost of hiring, number of passengers and speeds.'

A number of suggestions of this kind can be found in Appendix I.

With juniors, of course, it is important to direct their reading to the answering of factual questions and not to elucidating causes and effects.

In addition to the 'main set' of class history books and to reference books, it is valuable for every class to have sets of six or a dozen copies of some of the more reliable junior history books, to which children can turn when working individually or in groups. It is worth adding that teachers who are constantly seeking 'supplementary readers' can do worse than use sets of history books for those children who have acquired a taste for the subject. Many of these books contain exciting stories suitably written for juniors, though 'history readers' should never be used to practise the mechanics of reading with younger children.

THINGS TO DO

Once the period of history has been introduced and some basic information conveyed, interests begin to broaden, byroads present themselves for exploration, and the children want to be up and doing.

Throughout the Junior School, children must be given opportunities to understand history by making, drawing and finding out. It does not matter very much what the fashionable name for these opportunities happens to be—whether 'centres of interest', 'lines of development', 'activities' or, simply, 'handwork'. What does matter is that children shall learn by doing as well as by listening and reading, and that their teacher shall have done some planning to make this work worthwhile. While she will not wish to inhibit originality, she will have a clear idea of the learning value of her children's activities, since mere occupation with paint and paste, however engrossing, is not necessarily education. She will undoubtedly have to distinguish between those activities in which all the class can profitably join and others which small groups or individuals may perform.

NOTEBOOKS

It is not too much to say that, in the Junior School, the children's own history notebooks indicate, to a large degree, the value of the history which they are being taught. If they are neat, anaemic notes copied from the board, with meagre illustrations in pencil or, at best, crayon, so that all are exactly the same apart from the handwriting, then the history that the children are learning will be short-lived, if indeed it ever comes to life at all.

All juniors, especially in the first two or three years, delight in making illustrated books. They like to draw flint implements and Roman weapons, Saxon galleys and Tudor ladies; they like to re-tell stories of Boadicea or Queen Philippa at Calais, without too much correction of their spelling and grammar; they enjoy painting dramatic episodes, such as the stand on Senlac Hill, and making picture-strips about such people as Saint Alban, Becket and Cœur de Lion.

If these writings and their accompanying drawings are lively and original, they will contain a good many errors and anachronisms, which have to be treated with tact. Some errors are better allowed to pass, but others can be gently corrected so that a child's mistakes will actually lead to an increase in his historical knowledge. If the lake-dwellers are shown to be boiling a kettle upon their hearth-stone, or if the Saxons are seen to be wearing top-hats at Hastings, it is easy to suggest that a search be made for pictures that will show exactly the fashions of the time in headgear or culinary implements.

So much of this work laps over into the Art lesson, into English, Geography and Handwork, that it is futile to consider history as belonging merely to two half-hour periods on the time-table. When the 'project method' was very much more in vogue than it is today, there was a tendency to drag the project—'Houses' and 'Transport' were two especial favourites—into every aspect of school work, until teacher and children became heartily sick of it. Without going to artificial extremes, the teacher who is interested in history, finds a continuous carry-over of the history 'lesson' into art, craftwork, English, Geography and Scripture. There seems to be no reason at all why a school or a class should not develop a 'bias' towards history.

The individual notebooks, then, must be lively and colourful illustrated with pencil, ink, crayon, paint and cut-outs, for it is a great pity not to depart occasionally from the convenient crayon. The books themselves can be any size, from the usual exercise book to quarto, but, if they are any larger, children sitting next to each other will get in each other's way—really big books with their huge sugar-paper pages have to be the results of group work, where desks or tables are put together. If notebooks are smaller than about 8 in. by 6 in., the results will tend to be mean and fiddling. Whatever the size, the pages should be largely unlined, for which reason it is often best to make loose-leaf folders, with laced pages, and each with its gaily decorated cover. Into these books will go the facts, quotations, stories and anecdotes which children learn from their teacher and from their own researches.

It is often to be preferred that children make a number of history notebooks during the year, instead of only one. These can be loose-leaf or single-section sewn booklets. Each, consisting of only three or four sheets, will be devoted to one particular topic, the Normans, for instance, the Crusades, Tudor cooking or to subjects suggested earlier in the Teaching Notes. Sentences, quotations and stories will be written in them, with drawings, both original and copied or traced. For the youngest children, each page may have no more than a single sentence to its picture, but there should always be at least a title or caption describing the significance of each picture. Making a number of little booklets during the year not only caters for the junior's love of starting something new, but there is also the advantage that the child who made an unhappy start in his notebook will not be dogged with it for a very long time, he will always have the chance to produce one small masterpiece about some topic which has particularly caught his fancy, perhaps 'Games in the Middle Ages' or 'Elizabethan Sailors'. The coloured, decorated covers, clearly labelled, will enliven the history table, but it should always be clearly understood that the books will eventually become the child's own property. Teachers are well aware that to make something 'to take home' is usually to ensure that a great deal of effort will go into its making.

WRITTEN WORK

In addition to, and leading on from, the sentences describing their pictures, children may, from time to time, re-tell stories and happenings, even on occasion as the weekly 'composition'.

Topics and centres of interest will, however, normally supply the spur for most written work in history. Simple research by a group using the class or school reference library, will produce not only an illustrated book or frieze, but accounts of, say, the monastery time-table for a Benedictine monk, medieval punishments, Pepysian menus or the military equipment used at Waterloo.

There is, of course, always the danger of children copying out un-digested slabs of information, but this can be minimized by 'vetting' rough drafts and by insisting that each group displays the results of its research to the rest of the class, explaining each drawing or exhibit, and reading out its written accounts. There is also some risk that the inexperienced teacher, delighted that the class is busily occu-pied, will tend to be uncritical of what they produce.

It is often wise, therefore, to set a number of questions, topics or biographies which have to be explored and recorded, as has already been mentioned in connexion with reading for information. Even first-year juniors can describe how the Romans heated their rooms or decorated their houses; they cannot be expected to write a full account of St. Patrick's career, but they will describe how he was captured or how the monks employed themselves on Iona. Older juniors can be asked to describe, as if they were village children 600 years ago, their home, their own tasks and their father's work. A short list of suggested subjects of this kind is given in Appendix I.

It is often well to set a time-limit, at the end of which finished work must be displayed for class inspection, especially where time-tables are flexible and young teachers are given a proper measure of freedom in planning their work. This can vary from the elaborate model with its accompanying group book, to the little notebooks and gaily illustrated friezes upon which the written information appears with drawings, tracings and maps.

Few juniors are interested in making time-charts, but they delight in large display panels and friezes which illustrate their period of history. They like to arrange simple models and cut-outs of vehicles, armour, dress and houses. They enjoy making a manor-roll to which they fix the King's seal made from sealing wax, as much as they enjoy trying to write like a Roman boy with a stylus on damp clay or plasticine, and illuminating huge capital letters in the style of the monks.

The historical accuracy of the pictures from which children gain so much of their understanding of history, as well as the material for their drawings and models, is obviously of prime importance, and is discussed on another page. Since the illustrations of many school books are indistinct and suspect as regards accuracy, it is valuable for schools to obtain sets of postcards from the British Museum which cover a very wide range of historical subjects; postcards can also be obtained from the National Portrait Gallery of eminent men and women, as well as of kings and queens. Two other most useful sources are the Science Museum at South Kensington, for photographs of models of inventions, and the National Maritime Museum for ships throughout the ages. There are a great many local museums and places of historical interest which sell photographs that can be valuable source material for schools. There are in addition private concerns, such as aircraft companies, and public undertakings, the National Coal Board, London Transport and the General Post Office, for example, who can be extremely helpful. It is not perhaps out of place to add that the greatest care was taken to ensure the historical accuracy of the drawings in the four books of *Looking at History* (Black); the thousand drawings in these books can be used not only for drawings and tracing, but also for cut-outs, since a great many of them were specially drawn for junior children.

Some of the wall-panels and friezes, with their cut-out figures, vehicles and houses, may not possess very high historical value, but, especially with less-gifted children, they can be the beginning of a real historical interest.

These wall-panels need not always be primly flat; an amusing device is to cut a number of slits and to turn back the edges to reveal, say, a ship or a face, bursting out, so to speak, from behind the panel.

There is a good deal to be learnt from the technique of window-dressers in the big stores, as well as from comics, with their 'balloons' coming from the head of each character. One recalls a teacher effectively introducing the achievement of Columbus with a number of cut-outs of fifteenth-century gossips, whose 'balloons' indicated their sceptical comments on the quayside—'He'll fall off the edge of the world!', 'He'll never get to India that way!', 'They say his crew is made up of jail-birds', 'Did you hear that the Queen gave him the money?'

DATES

It is always a problem to decide how many or how few dates shall be included in the notes and written work of juniors. To some people, dates are a very prickly subject, but it is almost as foolish to ignore them as to over-emphasize the importance of learning them. On the whole, it is probably as well to attach a date to many of the more significant events and pictures in the children's recorded history, but it is unwise to insist upon them being learned by heart. The children, after all, are working within a limited period for a whole year, so those dates that are mentioned will not be selected from a vast period of history.

If children leave the junior school with some feeling for history as a process of time and knowing as many as six or a dozen landmarks, other than 1066, much will have been achieved; they might remember 55 B.C. and A.D. 410, 900 as the year of Alfred's death (though it is variously given as one or two years earlier), 1066 of course, 1215 (doubtful), 1381, 1415, 1485 (perhaps), 1588, 1603, 1649 (possibly), 1666, 1745, 1759 (possibly), 1815 and 1914.

But, in truth, dates do not matter greatly at this stage; indeed it is fatally easy to confuse even 'landmark' dates. The story is well known of the teacher who used a set of rhymes to help memorization:

'In fourteen hundred and ninety-two
Columbus sailed the ocean blue.'

Next day, he asked for the date of Columbus's great voyage, 'Fourteen, ninety-three, sir', came the reply from one boy.

'Fourteen, ninety-three? What was that little rhyme we learnt yesterday?' The answer came pat.

'In fourteen hundred and ninety-three
Columbus sailed the deep blue sea!'

That confusion is not confined to small boys may be shown by this recent and true story. A charming and effusive Inspector entered a classroom to find that the children were learning about the first Roman invasion.

'Ah,' cooed the Inspector, 'Julius Caesar? Now who knows exactly when he came to Britain? No one? Well, I'll tell you, it's a very easy date and a very important one to remember. Now, listen carefully, and say this together after me,

' "Julius Caesar came to Britain in 1066"!'

Needless to say, this story has enlivened staff-rooms many miles from the school in which the joyous mistake occurred.

DRAMATIZING HISTORY

Juniors, it is well known, have a keen dramatic sense, but while it would be foolish to ignore this natural tendency of young children to identify themselves with characters and scenes of the past, it is worth remembering that acting history is not an end in itself.

Full-length or one-act historical plays are rarely worth while in the junior school; and the best use of children's dramatic flair, as far as the learning of history is concerned, is in illustrating short scenes and ceremonies.

Acting of this kind is usually spontaneous and unrehearsed, though an episode which goes well may often be repeated and developed. Paying homage to the overlord, making Domesday Book inquiries, punishing the fraudulent baker with his short-weight loaf about his neck, Caradoc's last stand, ordeal by combat, the capture of Guy Fawkes and the activities of the Press Gang are some of the incidents that can be vividly acted or mimed, without any preparation, other than the lesson itself, and it will be readily appreciated that much of this spontaneous dramatization will be happiest with younger juniors who have not begun to develop self-consciousness. Though, in this connexion, much will depend upon the tradition of each school.

Miming is particularly effective, especially where a teacher is building up the habit and tradition of spontaneous acting. Queen Philippa pleading for the lives of the men of Calais, or Cromwell dismissing the Rump can be mimed with perhaps greater dramatic effect than would be achieved by speech. Once, however, they have caught the atmosphere, children can supply their own dialogue of astonishing dignity and vigour.

Though costumes and properties are by no means essential, it may be thought useful to have a few 'props' as part of the class equipment for history. One or two cloaks can add enormously to the spirit of the acting, and, if more than an old curtain is required, three yards of 54-in. material, cut in a semicircle, will make a much more lordly and ample cloak. The edges can be trimmed with cheap gold or silver ribbon though furnishing braid gives a more sumptuous effect, and the neck gathered and secured by a piece of dressing-gown cord. Darts on the shoulders improve the 'hang' of the material.

Cheap materials include hessian, both natural and coloured, butter muslin, old sheets, clean sacks and discarded curtain, though one must beware of contemporary patterns. Many large shops sell remnants at surprisingly frequent intervals and it is possible to buy pieces of brightly-coloured cloth and odd lengths of Bolton sheeting at reasonable prices.

Everyone, of course, knows how to make swords from card, or better, plywood, binding the broom-handle hilt with string; though silver or aluminium paint is good, black-lead rubbed on to the wooden blade gives a much more realistic metallic appearance. It can be varnished when used on cardboard plate-armour. Chain mail is made from openwork dishcloths or string vests painted with aluminium paint or dyed grey. Shields are made from heavyweight card, preferably not strawboard, with eyeletted holes to take wire handles, which, inside, are bound with adhesive tape or first-aid bandages. Heraldic devices or Crusaders' crosses are made of coloured gummed paper or, better, are traced round templates and painted on the shield, using, for once, oil paint or lacquer.

A stapling-machine is invaluable for quickly securing crowns, helmets and armour; most other fastening should be done by lacing, using the eylet-fixing tools and metal eyelets which are supplied by handicrafts firms. Lacing on sleeves and dresses, in particular, will supply an authentic medieval appearance.

Helmets have to be carefully copied from good drawings—those of Roman soldiers are usually made in two or three card sections secured together by brass paper-fasteners. Plumes can be made by cutting thin card into plume-like strips and running the open blade of a knife or cutting-out shears hard along one side of the card, which is thus made to curl quite realistically. The crowns of ladies' hats make good helmets, with cardboard visors added for knights, but left plain for the round steel caps worn throughout the Middle Ages; straw, of course, takes paint better than felt.

Many other simple devices are known to teachers for making effective properties for the short dramas of the classroom. The Roman toga, for instance, is a sheet but must be draped correctly—it was placed over the left shoulder, one end touching the floor in front, the rest hung down the back and was gathered up under the right arm and thrown over the left shoulder. Small boys, without any other costume, can be made into serfs by the wearing of the universal capuchon or hood, which is no more than a large triangular hood big enough to envelop the shoulders, with a slit for the face, so that the pointed peak hangs down the back.

A school set of the Iris Brooke Costume Books (Black) will provide an accurate source of information about details of historical dress, but the pictures of costume in *Looking at History* have been largely taken from those books and are in many cases simplified to help juniors in their 'dressing-up'.

Acting history can be a most valuable and vivid part of *learning* history, so long as that aim is kept in view. However, the size of most junior classes and the dimensions of their rooms are such that any dramatization has to be rapid and simple, if history rather than chaos is to be achieved.

MODELS

Because juniors delight in making things which they can see and handle and because it is now generally agreed that they learn most readily through themselves taking part in the business of learning, models of one sort and another must form an important part of history teaching.

Yet, there is always the temptation to allow model-making, like acting, to become an end in itself. Hours can be spent in making one splendid model—it may be the Norman castle, three feet high, complete with keep, bailey and drawbridge that really works, or the Elizabethan house, elaborately half-timbered with wings, gables and diamond-paned windows—but if only a handful of specially-selected children have contributed to this Open-Day masterpiece, then its value in teaching history may be less than if forty Norman keeps had been made from folded paper and paste.

Undoubtedly, there is sometimes much to be said for the elaborate model; it may represent a special effort for a special interest that has been aroused, it may mean a timely insistence upon a high standard of finish and it may represent the flowering of a special interest for one child or group. One recalls the backward class that made a splendid castle outdoors, using subsoil clay for the mound and real cement for the keep, but the class was small enough and the model big enough for everyone to take a share. There is occasionally the boy who spends weeks of his own time at home upon an accurate model of the *Golden Hind*, and his work is then worth a special corner to itself. But, in general, models should be simple, as representational as possible and they should not illustrate what can be effectively understood by reading and by pictures.

Historical models usually comprise the individual child's contribution—the wattle-and-daub hut, Viking ship, Tudor house or sedan chair, and the collective model, consisting of a scene or background upon which most of the individual models may be assembled.

As with acting and drawing, model-making will occupy a greater proportion of the younger junior's time than the ten- and

Sketch illustrating method of backing a collective model with a background picture attached to stiff card or wood.

eleven-year-old's. The older and more intelligent junior is advancing in his power to use and to understand written history, and he is also becoming more self-critical about his ability to draw and model realistically. Thus, while practical ways of learning are valid throughout the junior school and while great advantage can be drawn from increasing skills, older children will more readily work at times in groups where it is agreed that some are 'artists', 'illustrators', 'scribes', and others are 'readers' and 'co-ordinators'.

In the first year (seven and eight years), models usually include the many different homes which the children encounter—the cave, the herdsman's shelter, pit-dwellings, wattle-and-daub huts, lake-dwellings, Roman villa and shops, the Saxon hall. Weapons are another favourite—flint axes, made from short stout sticks and real flints if these are plentiful in the area, Roman swords and shields. There are also boats, such as the coracle and the long-ships, there are chariots and, of course, Stonehenge.

In the second year, models might include the castle and manor-house, the medieval village showing the three-field system, the medieval town or street and a monastery. Weapons, armour, hoods and heraldry are further subjects for profitable work.

In the third and fourth years, models often attain a high standard of finish. There are Tudor and Georgian houses, which help to make up street scenes, with the river, crowded with wherries, bum-boats and ocean-going galleons. There is furniture, from four-poster beds and chests to the spinet and elegant chair. There are stocks, pillory, the playhouse, and transport of every kind, from the heavy Tudor coach to the early aeroplane. There are puppets and dressed dolls, which girls dress with astonishing ingenuity.

These are some of the more obvious, but none the less important, activities that can usefully occupy children as they learn history. Only a selection would be attempted in any one year, and there are some notes and suggestions about models in Appendix II.

MODEL-MAKING

Before embarking upon any model, it is as well to reflect upon the

PART OF A WALLED TOWN. Made by 9-year-olds.

A TOWN SQUARE. With market cross, stocks, pillory and inn (houses made of card, with balsa-wood beams, doors and chimneys; roofs of corrugated card).

MEDIEVAL HOUSE IN ITS THREE SECTIONS. Two child's-size shoe boxes with "beams" of balsa-wood glued in position. Roof is made of two thick wedges of balsa-wood to which the foam-rubber thatch is pinned.

MODEL OF A MEDIEVAL HOUSE BY 9-YEAR-OLDS. An example of simplicity and speed in construction.

MODEL OF A SMALL GEORGIAN HOUSE, made by an 11-year-old boy of ply- and balsa-wood, with trees of bathmat foam rubber.

A WALLED TOWN. Made by 9-year-olds.

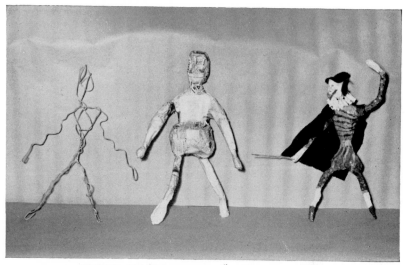

METHOD OF MAKING FIGURES (by 8–10 year olds).

The wire frame is covered with many layers of pasted newspaper—the centre figure will be a Tudor Courtier in padded tights. The last layer can be plain paper which is painted to resemble clothing, but in the last figure a girl has added a velvet cloak and hat—unfortunately she forgot the feet.

MODELS MADE FROM BALSA WOOD—by 10- and 11-year-old children.

DRESSED DOLLS MADE IN VARIOUS WAYS—heads of balsa wood, bodies of thin card or paper-covered wire. Dolls dressed by 10-year-old girls in dinner hours.

A GROUP OF STUART GENTLEMEN OUTSIDE AN INN (9–10 year olds)
The figures are made from tubes of cartridge paper painted with powder colours.

STUART PEOPLE (figures made quickly from cartridge paper, tubes, powder-colour and darning wool for hair!)

reasons for making it. Unless a model contributes to a child's understanding of history as well as to his pleasure in the subject, it is hardly worth all the organization and planning involved. As has been suggested, models merely for themselves, or as some evidence of progressive outlook on the part of the teacher, are a waste of time, and, whereas eight- and nine-year-olds will undoubtedly gain a great deal from making their model of a medieval village, intelligent eleven-year-olds may well derive a clearer understanding of eighteenth-century London through reading about it.

If the model illustrates an idea which can be quickly grasped, such as a Lake Village, it is not worth spending so long upon making the model that the children will become heartily sick of its protracted existence.

Nevertheless, though speed of construction and realism of appearance are essential qualities in a good model, it is important that a standard of finish is demanded which one can only define as appropriate for the age and ability of the children concerned. Slipshod models of ill-folded pastel paper are almost worse than no model at all.

MATERIALS

For models of any size, a firm base or frame is required. Old blackboards, shallow sand-trays, disused desks and tables are most useful (old desks need to be levelled up with blocks of wood screwed under the sloping tops, and, as a rule, covered with plywood or hardboard). Where, as in new schools, there is no stock of old equipment, a few trays of various sizes can be made cheaply with plywood or hardboard bases nailed to a frame of four strips of planed deal; if necessary, for large models, the corners can be strengthened by four triangular pieces of plywood.

One of the 'basic' materials for models is papier mâché; most teachers know how to make it, but for those who do not, it consists of a large quantity of newspaper torn up into small pieces and left to soak for a week in a bucket of water. Every day, the pulp is well squeezed and extra water added. When the pulp is formed, whitening powder and dry size (both obtainable from a paint shop) are well stirred in, until the pulp is ready to be shaped into hills or country-side or whatever the groundwork of the model may be. For large mounds, it is best to cover boxes with the papier maché, rather than use it in quantity. When shaped, it is well to smooth the pulp by brushing over with hot size or paste.

Plasticine or modelling clay can be obtained in many colours and is often to be preferred to papier maché, since it is far less messy to use, but it is more expensive until a good stock has been built up. Both take paint quite well, but Plasticine must first be brushed over with size, and ordinary powder paint is usually preferable to oil paints. Small objects can be modelled from pastry made from plain flour and water, with salt added to prevent the mixture from going mouldy. Polyfilla and plastic wood are immensely useful.

MAKING BUILDINGS

Buildings, of course, play a large part in historical models and they can be made in a variety of ways. Boxes of every size are always useful for the body of the house, to which a cardboard roof can be glued. If a number of boxes of the same size is available, effective roofs can be made by cutting a box in half diagonally and attaching it to a whole box.

Very simple houses, especially for younger children, can be made by folding stout paper or thin card, and, with practice, houses of varying dimensions can be made.

Small houses for a large model, such as a medieval village, may be made of solid Plasticine or potter's clay, and an advantage here is that the roof can be thickened and shaped to represent thatch, without the trouble of sticking on other materials. The 'thatch' can be painted on the Plasticine or clay, when the latter is dry. Indentations in the material represent doors and windows.

Stonework for buildings and walls can be imitated by a stiff mixture of grey powder paint or by covering the cardboard sides with a thin layer of grey or painted Plasticine. However, the most effective way of imitating stone is to make a mixture of real cement and fine sand in equal parts (this can also be bought ready-mixed and dry, in small bags). The wet cement is painted over the cardboard or

Plasticine walls, and the outlines of stone blocks marked with a sharpened piece of wood.

On Tudor houses, coarse wallpaper can represent roughcast, and timbering is shown by marking with a thick soft pencil. Thin strips of balsa wood or wide pipe-spills can be used for the same purpose, but they must be glued into place. Brown gummed paper seldom looks effective when used to indicate beams, since it tends to curl and peel away, besides being shiny. Brickwork has to be painted the right shade of red, though toyshops often keep printed paper of this kind.

Thatch is by no means easy to imitate. Split milk-straws and raffia take a good deal of managing and fixing into place. It is best to glue or sew them on to a piece of thin card which is bent over and glued to the roof. Long green grass can be similarly sewn on to thin card and trimmed with scissors; the grass soon dries to a realistic thatch colour. Tiled roofs are made from flattened corrugated card.

VARIOUS MATERIALS

Trees and hedges are made from loofah dyed or painted green and cut to suitable shapes and glued to the base, or, in the case of trees, to sticks which are inserted into the Plasticine or clay of the 'ground'. Fields are usually made by painting the base green, yellow or brown, but thin terry towelling, dyed by dipping in powder colour or cold-water dye and fastened down to the base, is very effective.

Roads are painted or are made of thick cement wash, into which tiny stones from road gravel can be set for Roman roads. Cobbles can be imitated by scattering small round seeds, such as hemp, on to cement.

Small figures, to add realism to models, are seldom satisfactory if made from Plasticine. Pipe-cleaners or wire can be shaped into a figure, leaving a loop of wire for the head. Cover the figure with lint or cotton wool and then wind adhesive tape all over. For the head and face, cover the wire loop with a little piece of flesh-coloured stocking and bind round the neck with cotton. These little figures can be painted or, rarely, dressed.

For larger figures, and for a display of costumes, girls show great skill in dressing small dolls and puppets. When a suitable doll cannot be found and the costume itself is of prime importance, a frame to display the dress can be made from basket cane and wire, which gives an authentic 'museum air' to the headless figures. Where a whole series of dressed dolls illustrate changes of fashion, they will be seen to much better advantage if all are made to stand up, either by placing the skirts over a pencil stuck into a thick base of Plasticine or clay, or by using supports of stout wire which have been stapled down on to an old piece of board.

While it is true that great ingenuity and skill can be employed in making models, it is worth repeating that speed of construction and clarity of purpose are the chief aims. The long gallery of an Elizabethan house, for instance, can be effectively depicted by a long cardboard background, with each end turned at right angles; windows, window-seats and tapestries are painted and pasted to this backcloth, against which are set the cut-out or modelled Eizabethan figures in various groups, and with pieces of furniture made from cardboard or, far better, from balsa wood. This kind of model takes very little time, and can realistically indicate the various use of the long room. Similar use of a background panorama, painted and devised by several children, can be used for medieval or Georgian street scenes. In front are arranged the houses, figures and vehicles made by the whole class. Elaborate diorama with glass fronts are more suitable for the museum than for the classroom.

One of the problems of model-making is space and storage; ruthlessness is the only solution, for the model must be broken up as soon as it has served its purpose. Nothing is so dreary as the dusty, disintegrating model which no one can bear to dismember, and the model of last term, let alone the one made by last year's class, has little value to children who rightly want to be making their own version of the subject.

When breaking up a model, it is worth taking care to preserve some of the basic materials for further work. Infants' counting sticks,

Sketches of simple models for the History table. Background and sides of card with paintings pasted on; balsa wood or card furniture, traced or drawn figure cut-outs, mounted on card with flap hinge. (By 10 year-old children).

lengths of thin dowel rod and both square and triangular picture-framing rods can be used again and again. Old penholders and butcher's wooden skewers should always be collected. Paper-clips or clothes pegs are required to hold card in position when it is being glued. Pieces of mirror glass for use as lakes, and old picture-frames are always worth keeping.

In addition to boxes, round cardboard tubes, corrugated paper and wood shavings, there are many materials that should be preserved in labelled tins in the store-cupboard. A tin of silver sand is most valuable; dyed loofah and terry towelling are always retained for use on another occasion. Incidentally, towelling, dyed brown, makes an effective substitute for the fur which decorated so many medieval costumes.

Most schools nowadays keep a fair range of cardboards; generally speaking, '3-sheet' is most suitable for children who are using only scissors, and they should learn to run their scissors along the inside of bends in order to obtain sharp creases; '6-sheet' and heavy

'10-sheet' card must be cut by the guillotine or with knife and straight-edge.

There is really no limit to the list of materials which can be used and catalogues from E. J. Arnold and Dryad are full of suggestions; the successful model-maker is the person who uses everyday materials in new and ingenious ways.

PICTURES

For many years teachers lacked sufficient suitable pictures for their history teaching; the close print of textbooks was only relieved, every ten pages or so, by sombre photographs of church interiors or of well-known pictures, such as West's 'Death of Wolfe' and Paton's 'The Return from the Crimea'. There were, and still are, the pictures contained in publications such as *Pictorial Education* (Evans), which are usually well drawn and accurate, but, being for years almost the only reliable source for wall-pictures, have tended to become a monotonous feature of every classroom in the school and to make little more impact upon the children than the chocolate and cream walls to which they were pinned.

Today it is just possible that schools are beginning to suffer from too many pictures. Publishers, aware that history books must be illustrated if they are to sell, and also aware that good illustration is a costly business, have taken refuge sometimes in second-rate colour and third-rate artists. Indeed, they often have no choice in the matter, because the purchasing power of junior schools is still pathetically low.

In school books, colour at a low cost is not worth having, for it results in fuzzy or garish illustrations, which are repulsive and frequently inaccurate. Far better than cheap colour are good line-drawings which not only appeal strongly to children but often give a clear indication of the possibilities of the subject for modelling and for copying.

Accuracy in historical drawing for children is so important that it is surprising to find 'howlers' so blatant as that in a recent best-seller, which showed Boadicea driving her chariot back to front. From the writer's personal experience, it seems essential that the author of a history book and his artist should work very closely together. Indeed, the artist must either be interested in history or be prepared to endure close briefing. If, for instance, he is drawing the scene during the Great Fire, when Mr. Pepys was burying his wine, he must beware making the bottles look exactly like our twentieth-century containers for Rich Old Tawny, because English bottles had not attained that shape as early as 1666. When he draws Wat Tyler and the peasants storming across London Bridge, he has to remember that it was only the last section on the city side that could be raised against attackers. The rig of ships is a perpetual snare for artists, but too many appear in history books rigged in a manner that would result in a disastrous capsize!

When a vassal did homage to his lord, he laid aside his belt, dagger and sword, so pictures of homage should always show the vassal unarmed, especially as this very scene may be acted in the classroom. How often is a handsome, young Saladin seen meeting Richard I on battlefield or in tent, whereas, in fact, these heroes never met and Saladin was twenty years older than the English king!

Two of the more deplorable features of poor history pictures is their tendency to glamorize the past, and to snatch at children's superficial attention by highly-coloured and indistinct illustration. This is the technique of the comic and the popular 'annual', but clarity and accuracy are by far the chief qualities required in a school history book.

Yet pictures are essential; it is laborious to describe in words exactly what a battering-ram was, but a child can understand it at once in a picture. A recent history book devotes two pages to a careful description of a pit-dwelling, yet a good drawing and a short paragraph would do the job far more effectively.

THE USE OF PICTURES

There has been a school of thought which advocated that history pictures should almost always be reproductions of contemporary drawings. It is certain that those delightful peasants with their flails, and the coach-horses mounting the side of the page because they were going uphill possess, in their quaint and lively authenticity, an appeal to sophisticated minds. But a child is not a cultivated adult, nor did the medieval artist think or draw as his modern successors do. Literal-minded children often find these pictures both confusing and silly; worse, their own strong sense of realism leads them to suppose that folk in 'the olden days' were incompetent and simple-minded. Contemporary illustrations have a real value in teaching history, but they should not be used too generously without explanation, and they are often better re-drawn by a good artist.

Photographs of museum exhibits, of ancient churches and monuments can be extraordinarily dull. Unless the photographs are brilliantly reproduced, a child always prefers a clear drawing of the same subject. Nevertheless, a collection of museum postcards is most valuable as a source of reference, especially for children's drawings and models.

Most teachers realize that pictures should always be placed at about the eye-level of a child, but it is all too common to find class-room pictures placed at height suitable only for men over six feet tall! The provision of pin-boards on the walls of classrooms, usually at the back of the room, has much improved in recent years, but it sometimes has led to such a profusion of pictures that a child absorbs little knowledge from them. It almost seems as if a teacher says, 'We are going to "do" the Tudors this term; very well, let us ransack the staff-room files for every picture we can find which has any connexion whatever with the period. Then we can cover up that bare wall, economizing with drawing-pins, by overlapping the dog-eared edges.'

This haphazard use of pictures has so little value that it is worth resolving never to put up any history picture which is not pleasantly backed, and which has not been separately looked at and discussed with class or group. It is sometimes well to surprise the class by pinning-up one or several pictures when they are not present, and attaching to each a label with questions, 'What is the servant holding in his right hand?', 'What is being sold at the booth outside the wall?', 'How many different tradesmen can you see?' In an age when pictures are always demanded but seldom examined, it is useful to encourage children to look closely and with discrimination.

When discussing and assessing the value and use of pictures, it is interesting to recall that Professor M. D. Vernon of the Department of Psychology, University of Reading, has carried out an investigation into the 'Instruction of Children by Pictorial Illustration', which is described in the *British Journal of Educational Psychology*, November 1954. Two studies were carried out with children aged eleven and twelve years and the results showed no decisive evidence that pictorial illustrations produced anything more than a very limited addition to the information given by the written text. Many objections to this finding will at once spring to the mind; there are the ages and intelligence and reading skills of the children to be taken into consideration, as well as the quality of the pictures and the interest of the text. Moreover, in junior schools, younger children are much more attracted to pictures than are eleven- and twelve-year-olds. Nevertheless, when all is said, it is salutary to have some evidence, however vague, that pictures may be a somewhat overrated aid to learning, though many will aver that it merely confirms their view that effective learning depends more upon the teacher than upon any other factor.

FILM-STRIPS

There is an increasing number of film-strips suitable for junior schools, though there are still too many schools which lack either the equipment or the facilities to use film-strips to advantage. Most teachers feel that these visual aids should be used sparingly and, as a rule, to illustrate a particular topic in the history course.

It is worth saying that the episcope and the epidiascope which can project images of pictures from the pages of a book are rarely supplied by Local Authorities to primary schools, as distinct from secondary schools; yet it is probable that this kind of projection would be even more acceptable to teachers than the film-strip projector. Much, however, remains to be done in the provision of screens and of blacking-out classrooms, since daylight projection, the alternative to the prohibitive cost of curtaining large rooms, still of doubtful value for classes of forty children.

RADIO

The B.B.C. Broadcasts to Schools have for some time included four history series of which one or more may be used in the junior school. 'Stories from World History', being mainly for ten-year-olds, is probably more widely used than 'History I' for younger pupils in the secondary school and 'History II' for children aged thirteen and over. There is also 'How Things Began', a programme of very high quality about pre-history, which is suitable for children of eleven years onward.

Clearly, there is small provision for the whole body of the junior school, and, within the restricted limits of time for school broadcasting, much more might be done for the eight-to-ten-year-olds. However, the question arises how far broadcast lessons can be used to help history teaching in the primary school.

The disadvantage of these broadcasts is that no amount of planning by the B.B.C. can devise a series of broadcasts which is likely to fit a school syllabus, though, when every allowance has been made, there do seem to be some extraordinary ideas of what are suitable topics for junior school history.

Nevertheless, the general standard of schools broadcasts is so high that it is always worth examining the term's programme in order to select those broadcasts which will fit in, to a reasonable degree, with the general plan for the class.

There is much value to be gained from children and teacher listening together to dramatized stories, which may not only serve as an introduction or a recapitulation of class work, but as a subject for discussion and criticism. In addition, it is one more way of helping children to realize that history is a subject which exists for people who dwell outside classrooms!

Though the amount of school time which can be given to history has to be jealously guarded, it is well worth making occasional use of history broadcasts which lie outside the syllabus of the top year; this is especially true of the series 'How Things Began'.

While preparatory and follow-up work are often necessary for these occasional broadcast lessons, there is also a good case for sometimes letting the broadcast make its own impact, without any discussion at all.

REFERENCE BOOKS

The changed outlook of recent years upon the teaching of juniors even though they are still in their huge classes, has called for a wide range of junior reference books on every kind of topic.

Most teachers today encourage children to look things up for themselves, to use books for information and as the source of much of their written work. At a time when children are widely accused of being spoon-fed, teachers know that they are full of zest and enthusiasm for the business of beginning to stand on their own feet in the matter of learning.

Yet the urgent demand for reference books for juniors is still hardly catered for by educational publishers.

There is an abundance of material for secondary school pupils, though most of that is more suitable for the middle and upper forms of grammar schools, but there is remarkably little that has been written for juniors by people who teach them and understand their needs and limitations. Many so-called 'information' books and 'junior' encyclopaedias have appeared since the war, but almost all of them suffer from the same defect of trying to cater for an age-range of from ten to eighteen years. Nearly all, including even the invaluable Quennell books (though these were certainly never written for juniors), are far too adult in tone, in layout and vocabulary. What is needed in the junior school today, perhaps more than anything except smaller classes, is an abundant supply of well-illustrated, simply-written reference books, which are inexpensive, but stout enough to withstand robust use.

But, whatever the difficulties, it is essential that there should be a school reference library, with a history shelf, from which children and teachers can take individual books or sets of six or a dozen copies. Children should act as the librarians, for they will not only widen their knowledge of books, but they will prove to be rigorous taskmasters in the matter of tracking down books which go astray.

There are signs that publishers have become aware of the need for simple books of reference but too many of these 'information' series remain unsuitable in style and vocabulary for most nine- to ten-year-olds. A selection of reference books which are mostly within the grasp of older juniors is to be found in Appendix III.

HISTORICAL FICTION

Generally speaking, a great deal of historical fiction is written in a style which is too difficult for junior children, apart from the more able and interested eleven-year-olds. Therefore, it is best to do no more than to add historical stories to the class library, from time to time, bringing them to the notice of ten- and eleven-year-olds by a timely word of introduction and by pinning their dust-jackets to a display board. It will be found that they have a strong following among boys, but less appeal to most girls.

Many historical stories have serious defects which make teachers doubtful of their value; they often tend to confuse fact and fiction, to romanticize the past and to over-stimulate a child's imagination. They frequently apply twentieth-century standards of behaviour to periods of history where very different values from our own were held. This is a very much greater fault than using either archaic jargon or modern idioms. As one preface puts it: 'Please don't read this as a "history" book! It is an adventure story about people rather like ourselves.'

However, there are many children who like history and who want to read historical stories. Some publishers, notably Oxford University Press, go to great pains to ensure that their historical fiction possesses accuracy and literary value. A difficulty is that very little has been written for children younger than about ten years—though many adults will remember devouring Henty's books at a more tender age—and that early history has not so far attracted many writers. Nevertheless, it is very difficult to generalize about the capacity of the child who really enjoys history, and the following titles are suggested in the knowledge that they have been read and enjoyed by some juniors aged nine years and upward.

EARLY TIMES

The Axe of Bronze—Schmeltzer (Constable).
Fires of Revolt—Durant (Bell).
Bran the Bronzesmith—Reason (Dent).
Swords of Iron—Reason (Dent).
Hounds of the King—Treece (Bodley Head).
Legions of the Eagle—Treece (Bodley Head).
The Eagles have Flown—Treece (Bodley Head).
The Eagle of the Ninth—Rosemary Sutcliff (O.U.P.).
Warrior Scarlet—Rosemary Sutcliff (O.U.P.).
Bronze Eagles—Lowndes (Collins).
Alfred, King of the English—Oman (Dent).
Mist over Athelney—Trease (Macmillan).

MIDDLE AGES

Knight Crusader—Welch (O.U.P.).
Ransom for a Knight—Picard (O.U.P.).
Young Master Carver—Tring (Phoenix). (Reign of Edward III.)
The Gentle Falcon—Lewis (O.U.P.). (Princess Isabella.)
The Woolpack—Harnett (Methuen).
Adam of the Road—Gray (Black). (Minstrel in Middle Ages.)
He went with Marco Polo—Kent (Harrap).
Son of Columbus—Baumann (O.U.P.).
Ferry the Fearless—Oman (Pitman). (Boy who longs to be a knight—Richard I.)
Johel—Oman (Pitman). (Boy in Richard I's reign.)
Redcap runs Away—Power (Cape). (Minstrel.)
Chronicles of Robin Hood—Sutcliff (O.U.P.).
Jockin the Jester—Moray-Williams (Chatto).
The Gauntlet—Welch (O.U.P.). (Feudal England—Barons.)

TUDOR AND STUART TIMES

Young Drake of Devon—Dawlish (O.U.P.).

He fought for his Queen—Willard (Heinemann).

The King's Beard—Wibberley (Faber).

Cue for Treason—Trease (Phoenix). (Elizabeth's reign.)

Grey Adventurer—Trease (Phoenix). (Civil War.)

The Wonderful Winter—Chute (Phoenix). (Eliz. London.)

Columbus Sails—Hodges (Bell).

The Escape of the King—Lane (Evans). (Charles II—Worcester.)

He went with Christopher Columbus—Kent (Harrap).

Armourer's House—Sutcliff (O.U.P.). (Tudor period.)

Brother Dusty Feet—Sutcliff (O.U.P.). (Tudor period.)

The Queen Elizabeth Story—Sutcliff (O.U.P.).

Simon—Sutcliff (O.U.P.). (Civil War.)

Down Ryton Water—Gaggin (Harrap). (James I—*Mayflower*.)

Farthing Family—Graveson (Bannisdale). (Quakers—Plague.)

The Flag from the Isles—Dickinson (Cape). (Flodden.)

Fortune My Foe—Trease (Methuen). (Sir Walter Raleigh.)

FROM GEORGIAN TIMES

Hornblower Cadet Edition—Forester (Joseph). (Nelson's times.)

The Golden Quest—Crisp (Bodley Head). (18th C. sea-faring.)

Blow the Man Down—Vipont (O.U.P.).

Clippers to China—Knight (Macmillan).

The House in the Sea—Wood (Harrap). (Eddystone.)

Young Harry Tremayne—Pertwee (O.U.P.). (Napoleonic Wars.)

Blackadder—Cross (Muller). (Pirates—including Trafalgar.)

He went with Captain Cook—Kamm (Harrap).

Peril on the Iron Road—Carter (Hamilton). (Railways, about 1850.)

The Grey Pilot—MacVicar (Burke).

The Escape of the Prince—Lane (Evans). (Charles Edward Stuart.)

Splendid Journey—Morrow (Heinemann). (American pioneers.)

Fearless Treasure—Streatfeild (Joseph). (Social history.)

Captain of Dragoons—Welch (O.U.P.). (Marlborough.)

Captain of Foot—Welch (O.U.P.). (Peninsular War.)

Path-through-the-Wood—Wilson (Constable). (19th C. nursing.)

This is a selection from the large number of historical novels for children which have been published in recent years; old favourites by such writers as Henty, Buchan, Marryat and Kingsley have not been included and many excellent stories have been missed or left out. Additional titles can be found in *Historical Fiction, 1957* (National Book League), *School Library Books, Non-Fiction, 1965* (N.B.L.), *Historical Novels*, Helen Cam (Routledge & Kegan Paul), *Four to Fourteen*, Lines (Cambridge) and *Handbook for History Teachers* (Methuen).

★   ★   ★

The suggestions in this little book about teaching history to juniors are made, in all humility, in the hope that they may be of some service, especially to students and young teachers, and perhaps also to older teachers who are not specialists in the subject. Possibly the author may best acknowledge his debt to the Ministry of Education Pamphlet No. 23 by concluding with a quotation from its pages, which seems to sum up exactly the task and the aim of teaching history to juniors:

'A good many alternatives to "straight" history have made their appearance in the last decade or two, though not so many have survived. Perhaps the most important thing about them is that they serve as a constant reminder to the history teacher that he must keep his subject alive and vivid. If he does that, facing squarely the need for ruthless selection, remembering that it is more important to know what to leave out than what to put in, then he need not worry too much about whether he is proving or explaining some contemporary proposition. He will be educating his pupils, giving them principles from which later on they will be able to judge contemporary matters when they are called upon to do so. . . . Yet it is often best to let history tell its own story; to tell its story even when we cannot point directly to a purpose or a moral. It's a very good story; what it needs most is good telling.'

APPENDIX I

A SHORT LIST OF SUGGESTIONS FOR WRITTEN WORK IN HISTORY

(Usually to accompany drawings and models, to stimulate 'finding out', and also as part of children's work in English.)

FIRST YEAR

1. Single sentences describing drawings:
   e.g. 'Early man lived in the forest on the banks of a river';
   'Early man made his home in a cave';
   'He made a flint axe';
   'Cave man made a fire. The children kept the fire alight.'
   (See *Looking at History*, Book I.)
2. Suppose you are a boy at Glastonbury, tell how the Lake-Village was made.
3. 'Do you not know, Briton, that you must shortly die?' asked the Emperor. Tell the rest of the story of Caractacus.
4. How did the Romans heat their houses?
5. How did they decorate the floors and walls?
6. You escaped from the pirates. Write one sentence telling how they captured Patrick.
7. Why did St. Augustine go to Britain?
8. Write a sentence about Iona.
9. 'Once upon a time, there was a cowherd named Caedmon...' continue the story.
10. Where did the Northmen come from?
11. Write down the names of any towns which have Danish names. (Do they end in -thorpe, -wick, -by, -car?)
12. Write down some reasons why Alfred was called 'The Great'.

SECOND YEAR

1. You are a Saxon who fought at Hastings. Tell how the battle ended.
2. Why did William I build castles?
3. Suppose you are a page at the Castle, describe the Great Hall and tell where people sit at dinner.

4. You are Rob Plowman, a villein's son living in a village; describe your father's work and tell about your own jobs.
5. Make a list of the jobs of the men in your village.
6. Suppose you are a novice at the monastery. Describe how you spend your day.
7. Explain: prior, abbot, dormitory, almoner, cloisters. Find out the names of the chief parts of a monastery.
8. What was the pillory? Tell about punishments.
9. Dick Martyn, a mercer's apprentice, describes the street he lives in.
10. Find out the meaning of: a mummer, friar, pilgrim, squire, guild, leper.
11. Make a list of the food and drink on the baron's table.
12. (a) Make a book called 'People of the Middle Ages' and write a sentence about William the Conqueror, Richard the Lion Heart, Robert Bruce, The Black Prince, Henry V.
   (b) Make another book called 'People who helped Others' and write a sentence about St. Margaret, Queen Philippa, Chaucer, Caxton.
13. You were an archer at Agincourt. Tell how the battle was won.
14. Tell what happened during the Peasants' Revolt.
15. Make a little book about John Staple, Wool Merchant. Describe your house, your new bed, kitchen, parlour, your clothes and food.
16. Find out where Caxton set up his press, the name of his house, the titles of any of his books, and the kings who came to visit him.
17. Why did pilgrims go to Canterbury? Describe Chaucer's adventure with the robbers, as he himself described it to the King.
18. What lessons would you have to learn in the Middle Ages as (a) a boy or (b) as a girl, if your father was a noble?
19. Tell how the medieval peasants built their homes.
20. Make a list of games in the Middle Ages.

THIRD YEAR

(Much of this written work will occur in 'English' lessons and can either be done in the History Notebook, in a separate book, or best of all, in several smaller booklets.)

1. In your booklet, 'Tudor Homes', write a sentence about the framework of a house, chimneys, ceilings, floors, windows. Begin 'I am Roger (or Marion) Freeman, my new house is . . .'
2. What was the long gallery used for?

3. Write a paragraph about furniture in Tudor times.
4. You are a scullion boy or girl in a Tudor kitchen. Describe the meals you help prepare. Mention breakfast, dinner and 'rere supper'.
5. In your book, 'Tudor Seamen', write a paragraph about Cabot, John Hawkins, Frobisher, Davis, Grenville, Raleigh, Gilbert, saying why each is remembered.
6. What did the 'Merchant Adventurers' do? Find out about Chancellor and Fitch.
7. Make a list of some reasons why Francis Drake deserves his great fame.
8. Write a short essay called 'A Seaman's Life', telling of the hardships at sea, but say why you still sail with Drake.
9. Suppose you are a newspaper reporter in 1588, write a short 'stop-press' notice about the Armada.
10. Write a column called 'Fashion Notes' for your book about 'clothes'.
11. Describe the 'Globe' as if you have just visited it.
12. How did people travel in Elizabeth's reign? Mention the dangers and difficulties.
13. Pretend you are Dan Wakefull, Watchman, who lives on London Bridge. Tell about Elizabethan London, especially the sights and scenes which are very different from modern London.
14. Find out as many things as you can which were *newly discovered* in Tudor times. Include countries, food, materials for houses, amusements, weapons, travel.
15. In your book, 'Stuart People', write a paragraph about Guy Fawkes, William Harvey, John Bunyan, John Milton, Prince Rupert, William Penn.
16. Write a letter from one of the Pilgrim Fathers to a brother who stayed at home. (You can be Patricia Mullen or John Alden.)
17. Princess Anne tells how she and Sarah Churchill escaped from the palace.
18. How did the Great Fire start? How was it put out?
19. Who were these people: Inigo Jones, Christopher Wren, Grinling Gibbons?
20. Suppose you went to dinner with Mr. Pepys. Describe what you ate and how he amused you.
21. Why did people use the River Thames as a highroad? Describe some of the sights, boats and people you might see on the river.
22. Make a booklet called 'How People enjoyed themselves in Charles II's Reign'. Write about games, sports, music, racing, plays, parks.

23. Describe the differences in the dress of Mr. and Mrs. Pepys and Mr. and Mrs. Plainman, a Puritan couple.
24. Write a sentence about Mary Queen of Scots, Lady Jane Grey, Mary Tudor, Queen Anne, and Queen Mary, wife of William III.
25. Would you have been a Jacobite? Why did some of the Scots (but not the English) help Bonnie Prince Charlie? Find out any songs about the Prince and write out one in full.

FOURTH YEAR

1. Make a book called 'Good People' and write down why these are remembered—John Wesley, Wilberforce, John Howard, Elizabeth Fry, Florence Nightingale, Lord Shaftesbury, Robert Owen, Baden-Powell.
2. How did John McAdam make his roads?
3. Write an account of your journey from London to Dover by stage-coach.
4. Explain the use and the appearance of these vehicles—post-chaise, gig, phaeton, whiskey, sulky.
5. Describe how you, 'Gentleman Jack', held up the Norwich coach.
6. Write an article called 'Town Travel in Georgian Days' mentioning the sedan chair, hackney coach, first omnibus and steam coaches.
7. 'Caught by the Press Gang!'
8. In your booklet 'Georgian Homes', write notes on the appearance of the houses, windows, an Adam room, furniture, fireplaces.
9. Tell how Wolfe captured Quebec.
10. Explain how the soldiers at Waterloo fired their guns. Make a list of a soldier's equipment.
11. Find out as much as you can about duels, prize fights, and cock-pits.
12. 'Cricket in 1750.'
13. Who were the Bow Street Runners, 'Peelers', 'Charlies'?
14. In your book called 'Early Railways', find out the names of some early locomotives; mention Murdoch, Trevithick, Stephenson, the Rainhill Trials, gauges and signals.
15. Write a short History of the Bicycle.
16. Find out the story of *The Great Eastern*.
17. In your book about 'Ships' include an article about the Clippers.
18. Make lists of street cries and street traders in Queen Victoria's reign.
19. Why were men like Lord Shaftesbury, Dickens and Doctor Barnardo sorry for poor children in London and big cities?

20. Mention some of the reasons why Captain Cook was a great sailor and a good captain.
21. In Nelson's day, boys and even girls went to sea. Suppose you were on the *Victory*, describe the appearance of Lord Nelson. Say why you think he is remembered as our greatest sailor.
22. Why did Livingstone spend most of his life in Africa?
23. Tell, in her own words, how Elizabeth Garrett became a doctor.
24. You were in Mafeking during the siege; describe how Colonel Baden-Powell defended the town.
25. How did the Boy Scout movement begin?
26. Tell the story of the Wright brothers.
27. What discoveries did these men assist—Henry Ford, Edison, Marconi, Friese-Greene, Benz, J. L. Baird, Nuffield.
28. For a book called 'Pioneers of the Air', find out about Colonel Lindbergh, Amy Johnson, Kingsford Smith, Bert Hinkler.
29. Describe an incident in the life of Winston Churchill, or Group Captain Cheshire, V.C.
30. Make a list called 'Modern Heroes' and write about one.

APPENDIX II

SOME SUGGESTIONS FOR SIMPLE HISTORY MODELS

Note: Almost all these, and other, models can be based upon pictures in the four books of *Looking at History*, where, in many cases, pictures have been specially drawn with the requirements of model-making in mind. Quennell's *History of Everyday Things* series is, of course, a splendid source of accurate material for models. Helpful details are also to be found in *Handwork Methods in the Teaching of History*—Milliken (Wheaton).

FIRST YEAR

Cave-dwellers' Home

(It may of course be held that the idea of the cave home is so easily comprehended that a model is superfluous.)

(i) Using an oblong tray, make the underlying structure of a cliff with boxes. Coat with white Plasticine to simulate chalk, leaving gaps for caves; work pieces of stone into cave openings. Top of cliff and foreground are green, with loofah bushes and trees; use fine sand in cave mouths, with twig fires and pipe-cleaner figures.

(ii) If a larger cave is required to show interior, use stout cardboard box; crumple stiff wrapping paper into a cave-shape and fit into box, giving slight taper to roof and sides; glue to sides of box. When fixed, paint inside of cave with thick grey paint. Disguise box-shape by fixing sheet of card cut as cave-mouth. Fine sand and small boulders in cave; twig fire, cave-paintings.

Pit-dwellings

(Illustration p. 14, *Looking at History*, I.) Bank is made of earth or Plasticine; excavate circular pit with stout twig as centre-pole; walls of Plasticine cubes or real stones. Roof with circular piece of card, roughly thatched with real grass or moss, stuck to Plasticine layer.

Hill-fort

(P. 15, *Looking at History*, I.) Mound of earth, Plasticine or papier maché, with moat. Huts of clay or card, thatched; stockade of twigs or matchsticks; sheep and cattle pens with toyshop animals. Real grass drying on poles. Dew-pond of glass or mirror.

Model of Long Gallery; back wall is merely card strip fixed to back of table, with end-wall similarly fixed to end of table to enable ceiling to be placed on top and secured with Selotape. Balsa wood chairs, table and spinet; figures of covered wire.

Lake Village

(P. 23, *Looking at History*, I)—large disused picture-frame as base, with glass representing water; make central island of Plasticine as large as possible or cut out a turf about 2 in. thick, pressing in matchsticks as piles; include landing-stage and boats. Card, clay or Plasticine huts.

Roman Villa

This is a difficult model for younger juniors. It may be made in a square tray, with buildings of card on three sides and lower wall with central gateway along fourth side. The peristyle is a flap of card with short lengths of thin dowel-rod to represent pillars, set in Plasticine base. Walls are thickly painted stone-colour to hide joins and paper-fasteners; tiled roofs (flattened corrugated card) are grey or red. Half-timbering of second floor, windows and doors are marked in with thick pencil. Front walls of thick card or ply.

Roman Shop

An easier model, it may be merely a card box with opening cut out and counter placed across two-thirds of this opening. Walls and floors may be decorated with suitable patterns; wine-jars, bread, fruit, &c. made from 'pastry' and painted.

If a Roman street is built up, variety may be had by placing small town houses between the flat-roofed shops. These have tiled roofs, timbered upper floors, and projecting booth-like roof for porch or shop front, with pillars of dowel or counting-sticks. (See street scene, p. 37, *Looking at History*, I.)

'How the Romans heated their houses' can be shown by a simple model of a hypocaust; thick card floor, with mosaic design pasted on top, support floor on chunky pillars of clay, Plasticine or square strip wood. Include part of outer walls to show stoke-hole and vents in walls which conducted warm air upwards (these were hollow oval tiles—make four card rings and press into Plasticine at each corner of room).

Saxon Hall

This may be a straightforward model made from a box, with roof attached and thatched, and sides painted to represent wattle and daub between timber frame. Or a large open box may show interior of hall; in this case, attach, or cut, gable-ends and join across with beam of strip-wood; fix cross-beams (penetrate cardboard sides of hall) and wooden pillars each side of hall (pp. 45, 46, *Looking at History*, I). If model is large enough, interesting details may be added—central hearthstone (with charred twigs) dais, benches and tables of card or balsa wood, shredded raffia on floor, cattle-stall at end.

SECOND YEAR

Norman Castle

A familiar model which can be made in a variety of ways and sizes. The main feature is the keep on the mound; as a rule, make the corner turrets first and attach stout card walls with strong gummed strips, unless good boxes are available. Walls surrounding the bailey are best made of wood or interleaved matchboxes with crenellations cut from thin card pasted to top; all is painted grey or given cement wash.

Norman Great Hall

To show interior; make in same way as Saxon Hall, with roof left open; cut rounded windows, furnish with central fire or fireplace against wall, trestle-tables, &c. Paint piece of hessian or thin cloth with figures similar to Bayeux Tapestry for wall. Make paper canopy over dais. (P. 12, *Looking at History*, II.)

Manorial Village

On large tray or table-top, with three fields, two of dyed towelling, yellow, and third of corrugated brown paper. Mark strips. Common land painted green; loofah trees to mark forest edge. Church and manor house of cardboard (p. 14, *Looking at History*, II); villeins' houses of card or modelled from cubes of clay or Plasticine. Watermill with milk-top or card wheel.

Medieval Town

A group model to include many houses of clay or card, with timbering and flattened corrugated card roofs. Include one or two churches with square towers; leave space for town-square with cross; crenellated walls.

An alternative plan is to paint a long background picture with medieval skyline, mount on card and fix at back of table; arrange houses, shops and churches in huddled streets in front.

Monastery

Rather a complicated model for nine-year-olds, but there is a plan of a monastery in model-form on p. 31, *Looking at History*, II.

Simple models, in card, ply or balsa wood, such as stocks, pillory, archery butts, ducking-stool, peasants' cotts, a roasting-spit, Crusaders' shields and a medieval coach are interesting additions to the usual houses; examples of all these can be found in Book II of *Looking at History*.

THIRD AND FOURTH YEARS

(Though model-making may play a less important part in the history teaching of brighter children at ten and eleven years, it still has a considerable value, especially as children's skill with materials advances rapidly at this stage.)

Tudor Houses and Shops

With panoramic background scene, arrange half-timbered houses in a street. If they are arranged upon an inverted large tray, its side can be made to represent the water front, with river-steps, of the Thames. On the painted, or glass, river in foreground, wherries, a royal barge and galleons may be set. If a sufficiently large table is available, Southbank may be included, with its houses, Bear-garden and the 'Globe'.

A Long Gallery

This can be simply conveyed by painting a back-wall, showing diamond-paned windows, window-seats, &c., on stiff card, and arranging in front several groups of cut-out or wire figures, with balsa wood or cardboard furniture.

The Elizabethan Stage

A model may be made of the stage itself without including the rest of the theatre—see p. 39 of Looking at History, III.

Tudor Furniture

Tables, chairs, a sideboard, spinet, four-poster bed are some of the uncomplicated furniture of the period which can be made effectively from balsa wood, which is obtainable in various thicknesses and sizes, and which children can easily work with a penknife or guarded razor-blade. Special glue is supplied.

Horn-books

These were from $4\frac{1}{2}$ to 5 in. long; they may be cut from plywood, painted, covered with alphabet, Lord's Prayer, &c. and finally covered with sheet of cellophane.

Georgian House

This may be either the plain town house or the large country house, with its pillared front and stable wings. Cut front of house from single sheet of thin ply, glue similar gabled sides (glueing inner corner posts, since ply does not take nails well), roof with thin card, paint grey for slates.

Transport

A most popular subject for fourth-year children, who can now use a wider variety of materials and tools, including the fretsaw. Wheels are not easy, except for the thick wheels of the stage-wagon, which can be made from balsa wood or by shaping solid toy wheels; unless the metal wheels from toy carts and cannons are available, cut circular discs from thin ply and paint or ink spokes and hubs. Simpler forms of transport include the stage-wagon and coach (mail coach is difficult), post-chaise,

Shillibeer's omnibus and steam omnibus (p. 99, *Looking at History*, IV). Arrange vehicles in front of painted scene of Georgian houses.

'Puffing Billy' and the 'Rocket' may be made of balsa wood, with boiler from cardboard tube (e.g. badminton shuttle tube).

A sedan chair is easily made from balsa wood and has a hinged top (gummed cloth hinge inside) and curtains.

Early aeroplanes are made by enthusiastic boys using wire, silk, aluminium paint and the ubiquitous balsa wood.

Ships—hull is shaped from an oblong block of balsa wood and its flat bottom enables it to 'float' on a painted sea (though, being light, the hull may have to be tacked in position, or weighted), masts of thinnest dowel, halyards of florist's wire, sails of paper. Suggested ships—*Comet, William Fawcett, Britannia* of 1840, *Great Eastern, Victory.*

Tudor, Georgian and Victorian figures are also popular; these may be dolls or, better, wire figures, covered with strip after strip of pasted paper until shape is built up, and which are dressed or painted in appropriate style, girls sewing the dresses. Effective figures may also be made from thin-cardboard tubes of varying diameters, which are painted and fitted one inside another.

APPENDIX III

A BOOK LIST

(The following list contains almost all the books mentioned in the text. Those marked with an asterisk are suitable for a Junior Reference Library.)

*Puffin Books and Penguins:

    Early Man
    The Bayeux Tapestry
    Famous Ships
    A Book of Armour
    The Building of London
    Signs and Symbols
    Prehistoric Animals, &c.

Costume—Cunnington (Black).
Historic Costuming—(Pitman).
Costume Cavalcade—Hansen (Methuen).
Roman Britain—Fox (Lutterworth).
Everyday Life in Prehistoric Times—Quennell (Batsford).
Everyday Life in Roman Britain—Quennell (Batsford).
Everyday Life in Anglo-Saxon, Viking and Norman Times—Quennell.
A History of Everyday Things in England—Quennell, 4 vols. (Batsford).
Looking at History—Unstead (Black, 4 books).
People of the Past series—Pearce (ed.) (O.U.P.).
Looking at Ancient History—Unstead (Black).
A History of Britain—Unstead (Black):

    The Medieval Scene
    Crown and Parliament
    The Rise of Great Britain
    A Century of Change
    Britain in the 20th Century

Men and Women in History—Unstead (Black)

    Heroes and Saints
    Princes and Rebels
    Discoverers and Adventurers
    Great Leaders

Study Books series (Bodley Head).

History Bookshelves series (Ginn).
*Rockcliff New Project series (Rockcliff).
 Ancient Times—Breasted (Ginn).
 Prehistoric Britain—Hawkes (Chatto).
*Methuen's Outlines series (Methuen):
  The Story of Ships
  The Story of Aircraft
  Wheels on the Road
  The Story of the Kitchen
  Castles and Fortresses
  Early Explorers
  Railways for Britain
  The Vikings
  The Crusaders
  Roman Britain, &c.
British Railways Today—Ransome–Wallis (Black).
Railways—Fry (E.S.A.).
Railways—Allen (Blackwell).
Castles—Fry (E.S.A.).
Furniture —Harrison (E.S.A.).
Houses—Potter (Murray).
Simple Heraldry—Moncrieffe (Nelson).
Heraldry—Manning (Black).
Oxford Junior Encyclopaedia—Vols. IV, V, IX, XI (O.U.P.).
 London Through the Ages—Tickner (Nelson).
 English Social History—Trevelyan (Longmans).
Journey Through History, I & II—Gunn (Edward Arnold)
 A History of the English People—Mitchell & Leys (Longmans)
*'Then and There' series (Longmans):
  The Medieval Town
  The Medieval Village
  Roads and Canals in the Eighteenth Century
  The Railway Revolution, 1825–1845
  Elizabethan Court
  Elizabethan Ship, &c.
*'Looking at the Past' series (Chatto and Windus).
 'How They Lived' series (Blackwell).
 The Dawn of Civilisation (Thames and Hudson).

The First Book of Stone Age Man—Dickinson (Ward).
The Story of Your Home—Allen (Faber).
The Story of the Highway—Allen (Faber).
 A Miniature History of the English House—Richards (Architectural Press).
Days before History—Hume (Blackie).
History through the Ages—Firth (O.U.P.):
  Book III: *How People Lived*
  Book IV: *How People Travelled.*
*'People of the Past' series (O.U.P.).
The Roman People—Milliken (Harrap).
The Crusades—Thomas (Muller).
A Picture History of Britain—Hutton (O.U.P.).
*'Understanding the Modern World' series (Allen and Unwin):
  Your Hearth and Home
  Transport, Trade and Travel
  Yesterday: A History of Our Parents' and Grandparents' Times.
*'The Changing Shape of Things' series (Murray):
  Transport by Land
  Transport by Sea
  Transport by Air
  Houses.
A Valley Grows Up—Osmond (O.U.P.).
Castles—O'Neil (H.M.S.O.).
Arms and Armour in England—Mann (H.M.S.O.).
*Junior Heritage Books (Batsford).
This Wonderful World series (Harrap).
History Picture Books (Macmillan).
*Black's Junior Reference Books (Black):
  A History of Houses
  Travel by Road
  The Story of Aircraft
  The Story of the Theatre
  Travel by Sea
  Monasteries
  Furniture in England
  Arms and Armour, etc.
Abbeys—Gilyard-Beer (H.M.S.O.).
The Great Exhibition of 1851—Gibbs-Smith (H.M.S.O.).

SOURCE BOOKS—FOR CONTEMPORARY QUOTATIONS

Everyman's Library (Dent):
  Anglo-Saxon Chronicle
  Hakluyt's Voyages
  Captain Cook's Voyages
  Pepys's Diary.
Texts for Students (Sheldon Press):
  Village Life in the Fifteenth Century
  Travellers and Travelling in the Middle Ages
  Traders in East and West (East India Co., &c.)
  English Social Life in the Eighteenth Century.
**Picture Source Book, for Social History*—Harrison and Bryant 5 vol. (Allen and Unwin):
  They Saw It Happen (Blackwell)
  Documents of English History (Black)
Reference Books for Macmillan's History Class Pictures.
**Travel in England*—Burke (Batsford).
*A.D. History News Sheets—Newsom (Allen and Unwin, 1 vol.).
  The Pastons and Their England—Bennett (C.U.P.).
  Life in Shakespeare's England—Dover Wilson (Penguin).
*'Jackdaw' series (Cape).

SHORT STORIES OF PEOPLE

**People in History* series—Unstead (Black):
**Men and Women in History* series—Unstead (Black):
  1. Heroes and Saints
  2. Princes and Rebels
  3. Discoverers and Adventurers
  4. Great Leaders.
**A Child's Day Through the Ages*—Stuart (Harrap).
**Boys and Girls of History*—Power (C.U.P.).
**They Served Mankind* series—Taylor (Macmillan).
*Our Island Story—Marshall (Nelson).
**Scotland's Story*—Marshall (Nelson).
**Heroes of Welsh History*—Oates (Harrap).
**A Book of Discovery*—Synge (Nelson).
**The Age of Discovery*—Power (Putnam).
**Children's Book of Saints*—Lee (Harrap).

Children's Norse Tales (Harrap).
Lives of Great Men and Women series (O.U.P.):
  I. Social Reformers
  II. Great Explorers
  III. Great Inventors
  IV. Medical Scientists and Doctors
  V. Soldiers and Sailors.
Living Names series (O.U.P.).
History through Great Lives—Bellis (Cassell).
Kings and Queens in World History—Unstead (Odhams).
Lives to Remember series (Black).
Men of the Modern Age series (Bodley Head).
Men of Speed series (Newnes).
The Thrill of History—Magraw (Collins).
The March of Time—Horniblow and Sullivan (Grant).
The Kingsway Junior Histories—Power (Evans).
 Brief Lives series (Collins).
Men Who Changed the World—Larsen (Phoenix).
Famous British Engineers—Halward (Phoenix).
The Seven Queens of England—Trease (Dent).

TEACHING HISTORY

Ministry of Education Pamphlet No. 23, *Teaching History* (H.M.S.O.).
Learning Out of School—Harrison (E.S.A.).
Handwork Methods in the Teaching of History—Milliken (Wheaton).
Finding the History Around Us—Doncaster (Blackwell).
Guide to London Museums and Galleries (H.M.S.O.).
Handbook for Teachers (Methuen).

APPENDIX IV

A MODIFIED SYLLABUS
FOR ONE- AND TWO-TEACHER SCHOOLS

SCHOOL YEAR A

(For a one-teacher school or for younger class in two-teacher school.)

Cave-dwellers
Stone Age people
Pit-dwellings
Bronze Age farmers
Ancient Britons
The Romans
Roman soldiers
Caractacus
Agricola
Romano-British
   town life

St. Alban
Anglo-Saxon invaders
St. Augustine
St. Aidan
The Danes
King Alfred
Canute
William I
Norman castles
A manorial village

Richard I and
   Crusaders
Llewelyn
Bruce
Owen Glendower
The Peasants' Revolt
Henry V at Agincourt
Caxton
The Pastons
Life in the Middle Ages

SCHOOL YEAR B

(Second year's work in one-teacher school; a year's work for older class in two-teacher school.)

Thomas More
Tudor homes
Princess Elizabeth
Drake and Tudor
   seamen
Tudor amusements
Guy Fawkes
Rupert and Cromwell
Samuel Pepys
Stuart homes

Travel in town and
   country
Marlborough
Prince Charles
   Edward
Captain Cook
Ships and sailors
Georgian homes
James Watt
Stephenson

Lord Nelson
Steamships
Shaftesbury and poor
   children
Florence Nightingale
Victorian life
Captain Scott
Story of aeroplanes
Amy Johnson
Alexander Fleming

SCHOOL YEAR C

Third year in a one-teacher school or the second year's topics for 7–9's in a two-teacher school.)

Cave-dwellers
Stone Age people
 (New Stone Age)
Herdsmen
Stonehenge
Bronze Age people
Iron
Lake-dwellers
Celtic people
The Roman Invasion
Roads and towns
Boadicea

A Romano-British
 villa
St. Patrick
A Saxon village
St. Columba
Hilda
St. Cuthbert
Bede
Viking raiders
Ethelfleda
Edmund Ironside
Harold

Norman invasion
Hereward
Domesday Book
Norman homes
Queen Margaret
Hugh of Lincoln
A monastery
Becket
Wallace
Queen Philippa
Pilgrims and Chaucer
A medieval town

SCHOOL YEAR D

(Fourth year in one-teacher school or second year's work for 9-11 class in two-teacher school.)

Lady Jane Grey
Life in Tudor Times
Explorers
Capt. John Smith
Cabot
Chancellor
Raleigh
Philip Sydney
Shakespeare
William Harvey
The Pilgrim Fathers

Montrose
Stuart London
Clothes and furniture
William Dampier
Bunyan
Lady Nithsdale
Wolfe
Clive
The Coaching Age
Georgian Life
Wellington

Robert Owen
Arkwright
Elizabeth Fry
Town travel
Victorian homes
Livingstone
Motor-cars
T. E. Lawrence
Nuffield
Churchill
Cheshire, V.C.

APPENDIX V

TIME CHART

PRE-HISTORY, ROMAN OCCUPATION, SAXONS

APPROX. DATES	PERIODS AND PEOPLES	EVENTS	BACKGROUND
About 1 Million Yrs. B.C. to 10,000 B.C.	Palaeolithic Age (Old Stone Age).	Successive Ice Ages.	Crude flints. Cave-dwelling. Skin-clothing. Hand-Axes. Bone needles.
About 5000 B.C.	Mesolithic or Middle Stone Age	Glaciers retreated.	Cave drawings.
About 3000 B.C.	Neolithic or New Stone Age.	Longbarrow burial mounds.	Pit-dwellings. Polished stone tools.
About 2000 B.C.	Beaker folk in Britain.	Stonehenge.	Pottery and art. Agriculture. Horses.
About 1500 B.C.	Bronze Age.	Hill-fort warfare.	Early carts. Spinning & Weaving
1000– 500 B.C.	Celtic people arrived.	Brought iron.	Trade with Continent.
	Iron Age.	Glastonbury.	Celtic art.
200 B.C.	'The Ancient Britons'.	Belgic tribes invaded.	Tribal settlements & 'towns', in S.E. Britain.
55 B.C. 54 B.C.	Julius Caesar's Expeditions.	Nominal submission of Britons.	Infiltration of Roman goods and ideas.
	Further Belgic Invasions.		

DATES	RULERS	EVENTS AND PEOPLE	BACKGROUND
A.D. 43	Emperor Claudius.	Aulus Plautius defeated Caractacus.	Roman Occupation. First town and road building.
61	Nero.	Boadicea's rebellion.	
78–85	Agricola, Governor.	Druids destroyed. Invasion of Scotland.	Urbanization of S. Britain.
122	Hadrian in Britain.	Hadrian's Wall.	Villas in S. England.
304	St. Alban.	Persecution of Christians. Saxon raids.	Picts and Scots in North.
313	Constantine granted religious freedom.		
410	Capture of Rome.	Last Legions withdrawn.	Increasing Saxon raids.
400–600	'The lost centuries.' Angles and Saxons settle in Britain.	Hengist & Horsa.	British tribes put up a long and stubborn resistance for 200 years.
About 461		Death of St. Patrick.	
About 560		St. Columba in Scotland.	
597	Pope Gregory.	St. Augustine in Kent.	Spread of Christianity.
About 603 to 680	Kings Edwin, Oswald, Oswy of Northumbria.	St. Aidan. Synod of Whitby. Abbess Hilda and Caedmon. Bede (672–735).	Perpetual warfare, esp. against Penda of Mercia.
757–96	King Offa of Mercia.	Offa's Dyke.	Period of the Heptarchy (or Seven Kingdoms).
825	Egbert ('the Great') of Wessex, first King of all England (802–836).	Defeated Mercia at Battle of Ellanddune.	Saxon Open-field system of Agriculture.

DATES	RULERS	EVENTS AND PEOPLE	BACKGROUND
About 835	The Danes.	Viking raids.	E. Anglia, North and Midlands overrun. Christianity destroyed temporarily.
871–99 (or 900)	Alfred the Great, King of Wessex.	Inevitable clash with invaders.	
878		Guthrum defeated at Ethandune. Peace of Wedmore. *Anglo-Saxon Chronicle.*	Division of England into Danelaw and Wessex.
900–24	Edward the Elder.	Re-conquered Danelaw.	Gt. period of Wessex Kings.
925–50	Athelstan.	Conquered S. Scotland.	Spread of building and learning.
959–75	Edgar.	St. Dunstan.	Incr. power of the Church.
978	Ethelred the Unready.	New Danish raids.	Danegeld.
1013	Sweyn of Denmark.	Invaded Britain.	
1016–35	Canute.	Edmund Ironside fought him.	Canute ruled an Anglo-Danish Empire.
1042–66	Edward the Confessor.	Introduced Normans. Built Westminster Abbey.	Danes built towns and fostered trade. Use of stone for building.
1066	Harold. (son of Earl Godwin of Wessex).	Defeated Tostig and Harald Hardraada at Stamford Bridge (nr. York)	Wm. of Normandy prepared to invade.

THE MIDDLE AGES

DATES	MONARCHS	EVENTS AND PEOPLE	BACKGROUND
1066	William I.	Harold defeated at Hastings. Lanfranc, A. of Canterbury.	Tower of London and early Norman castles built. Norman abbeys and monasteries.
1069–70		North laid waste.	
1071		Hereward the Wake.	Continental feudal
1085		Domesday Book.	system.
1087	William II.	First Crusade— Jerusalem captured.	Rebellious vassals subdued. Normandy secured.
1099			
1100	Henry I.	Normandy invaded. H.'s son, William, drowned in 'White Ship'.	Strong kingship. Peace—growth of towns. Castles and manor houses built.
1135	Stephen (nephew of H. I).	Matilda (d. of Henry) contested throne. Civil War.	Misery and lawlessness. Trade and agriculture at standstill.
1154	Henry II.		Barons subdued. Law and order restored. Trial by Jury.
1170		Becket murdered.	
1187		Saladin c. Jerusalem.	
1189	Richard I.	The Third Crusade. Robin Hood.	Saladin tithe—towns gained charters & rights. Ship building.
1199	John.		Quarrel with Pope and Barons.
1203		Death of Prince Arthur.	
1215		Magna Carta.	Civil War.
1216	Henry III.	Stephen Langton. Hubert de Burgh.	Black & Grey friars. Weak rule and Civil war.
1265		Simon de Montfort.	First Parliament.

(Monarchs grouped as NORMAN KINGS from William I to Stephen; PLANTAGENET or ANGEVIN KINGS, early Angevins, from Henry II to Henry III.)

DATES	MONARCHS		EVENTS AND PEOPLE	BACKGROUND
1272	PLANTAGENET or ANGEVIN KINGS *later Angevins*	Edward I.	Llewelyn—Conquest of Wales. Scotland—Balliol—Wm. Wallace. Robert Bruce.	Century of 'Early English' Architecture—many cathedrals built or started—Ely, Wells, Westminster Abbey, &c.
1307		Edward II.		Inept government.
1314			Bannockburn.	Famine in England.
1327	PLANTAGENET or LATER ANGEVIN KINGS	Edward III.		Flemish Weavers came to England.
1338			100 Years War began.	
1340			Sea battle of Sluys.	
1346			Black Prince. Crécy.	Decisive use of longbow.
1347		Queen Philippa.	Siege of Calais.	
1348–49			Black Death. Wm. Langland, *Piers Plowman*.	One-third of population died. Rise in wages—Statute of Labourers—discontent.
1356			Poitiers. Chaucer 1340–1400. John Wycliff, Bible translated.	Wool. The Lollards. 'Decorated' period of architecture—Exeter, Wells, Salisbury, Winchester, Canterbury, &c.
1377		Richard II (deposed 1399).	John of Gaunt.	
1381			Peasants' Revolt, Wat Tyler—John Ball.	Peasants' lot gradually improved.

DATES	MONARCHS	EVENTS AND PEOPLE	BACKGROUND
1399	Henry IV (Bolingbroke).	Owen Glendower. Hotspur.	A troubled reign. Barons powerful and unruly.
1413	Henry V.	Harfleurs. Siege guns.	Persecution of Lollards.
1415		Agincourt.	Guilds powerful.
1422	Henry VI (succeeded at 9 mths. old).	Bedford.	
1431		Joan of Arc. The Pastons.	Gradual loss of French possessions.
1455–61	Queen Margaret (of Anjou).	Wars of the Roses. Warwick, King-maker.	Weak government—lawlessness.
1461	Edward IV.		Extravagant fashions.
1476		Wm. Caxton at Westminster.	
1483	Edward V. (murdered).	Murder of the Princes.	15th-C. 'Perpendicular' Style of
1483	Richard III.	Killed at Bosworth.	Architecture. Oxford and Camb. colleges.
1485	Henry VII.	End of Wars of Roses.	Barons' power on wane.

Monarch house labels (vertical): HOUSE OF LANCASTER (Henry IV–Queen Margaret); HOUSE OF YORK (Edward IV–Richard III); TUDORS (Henry VII).

THE TUDORS

DATES	MONARCHS	EVENTS AND PEOPLE	BACKGROUND
1485	Henry VII		Henry aimed to secure throne and weaken barons.
1487		Lambert Simnel.	
1492		Columbus' Voyage.	Security and trade improved.
1497		Perkin Warbeck. John Cabot—Newfoundland.	Royal wealth amassed.

DATES	MONARCHS	EVENTS AND PEOPLE	BACKGROUND
1509 1510	Henry VIII (m. Katherine of Aragon, Anne Boleyn, Jane Seymour, Anne of Cleves, Katherine Howard Katherine Parr).	Erasmus. Cardinal Wolsey. Sir Thomas More. Field of Cloth of Gold.	Hampton Court— use of brick. Period of domestic building through 16th C.
1520			
1530		Divorce of Katherine.	
1535		Execution of More; of Anne Boleyn.	The Reformation.
1536–39		Destruction of the Monasteries. Thomas Cromwell. John Knox. Cranmer.	
1547	Edward VI.	Somerset, Protector. Richard Chan- cellor.	Mass abolished. English Prayer book.
1553	Mary (m. Philip of Spain).	Lady Jane Grey executed. Cardinal Pole.	Latimer, Ridley Cranmer burnt.
1558 1558	Elizabeth I.	Loss of Calais. Wm. Cecil. Mary, Q. of Scots.	First coaches in Eng- land. Enmity with Spain.
1577–80		Drake sailed round world.	Increasing trade and exploration.
1583 1586		Gilbert drowned. Sir Philip Sidney died of wounds.	Growth of in- dustry.
1588		Armada: Drake, Hawkins, Howard, Frobisher.	Breakdown of Feudal System. Sheep-farming and end of monasteries caused distress and
1599		Raleigh and Gren- ville colonizing Shakespeare at the 'Globe'.	unemployment. Music, poetry and drama flourished.
1601		Treason of Essex. Poor Law.	
1603	James I.		

THE STUARTS

DATES	MONARCHS	EVENTS AND PEOPLE	BACKGROUND
1603 1605	James I.	Gunpowder Plot.	Puritans & Catholics rebuffed.
1617 1620		Raleigh's last expedition. Pilgrim Fathers sailed in the *Mayflower*.	Growing power of Parliament.
1625	Charles I.	Inigo Jones. Archbishop Laud. John Hampden.	King's shortage of money. Ship Money.
1642 1644 1645		Civil War. Edgehill. Rupert. Cromwell. Marston Moor. Naseby. Montrose in Scotland.	King and Parliament.
1649	The Commonwealth. Cromwell. The Protectorate.	Execution of Charles. Irish Campaign. War with Holland.	John Milton. Navy strengthened.
1660 1665 1666	Charles II.	Sam Pepys. Great Plague. Fire of London. Christopher Wren. John Bunyan. Grinling Gibbons.	'Renaissance' or 'Stuart' period of architecture, developing into 'Classical'. Ship-building. Dutch Wars.
1685	James II (abdicated).	Monmouth's Rebellion.	Appointment of R. Catholics. Army on Hounslow Heath.
1689	William III and Mary.	War against Louis XIV. War in Ireland.	

DATES	MONARCHS	EVENTS AND PEOPLE	BACKGROUND
1702 1704 1707	Anne.	Duke of Marlborough. Duchess Sarah. Blenheim. Union with Scotland.	England prosperous. Coffee houses. China-ware, porcelain and furniture fashionable. London mobs. Agriculture advanced.
1714	George I of Hanover.		

THE GEORGIAN PERIOD

DATES	MONARCHS	EVENTS AND PEOPLE	BACKGROUND
1714	George I of Hanover.	'The Fifteen'. South Sea Bubble. Sir Robert Walpole.	Supremacy of Whigs, a landowning aristocracy.
1727	George II.	War of Austrian Succession.	
1743		B. of Dettingen.	Rivalry with France.
1745		Jacobite Rising— Charles Edward.	John Wesley preaching.
1756–63		Seven Years War. Wm. Pitt.	
1757 1759		Robt. Clive— Plassey. Jas. Wolfe— Quebec. Hawke—Quiberon Bay. Brunswick— Minden.	Founding of British Empire and Naval supremacy.

DATES	MONARCHS	EVENTS AND PEOPLE	BACKGROUND
1760	George III.		Dr. Johnson and his Circle.
		Treaty of Paris.	
		Stamp Act—taxing of colonies.	Coffee houses. Sedan chairs.
1776–83		War of American Independence— Geo. Washington.	James Watt. Arrival of Steam-power. Improvement of farming.
1779		Captain Cook's death.	Gracious domestic architecture: Robt.
1793		War with Revolutionary France. Pitt the Younger. Napoleon.	Adam, Wm. Kent, Chippendale, Hepplewhite, Sheraton.
1805 1815		Nelson, Trafalgar. Wellington. Waterloo.	Heyday of Coaches and Carriages. Growth of mechanized industry.
		Trevithick. Wilberforce.	Steam locomotive. Steamships.
1820	George IV.	Eliz. Fry. Stockton and Darlington Rlwy. Rainhill Trials. Geo. Stephenson.	Regency styles. John Nash. Gothic revival. Shillibeer's Omnibus Hansom Cab.
1830 1832 1833	William IV.	Faraday. Reform Bill. Abolition of Colonial slavery.	Growth of Railways. Factories and Slums. Dickens's *Pickwick Papers*.
1837	Victoria.		

VICTORIAN ERA AND FIRST HALF OF TWENTIETH CENTURY

DATES	MONARCHS	EVENTS AND PEOPLE	BACKGROUND
1837	Victoria (m. Albert 1840).	Melbourne. Peel. Famine in Ireland.	Social distress. Rising population, unemployment.

DATES	MONARCHS	EVENTS AND PEOPLE	BACKGROUND
1840		Penny Post— Rowland Hill. Palmerston.	Industrial Revolution. Agriculture depressed.
1847		Factory Acts. Lord Shaftesbury. Joseph Lister— antiseptics. Robt. Owen.	*Laissez-faire.* Emigration to colonies. Women and children in mines and factories.
1851		Great Exhibition.	Rise of Trade Unions. Free Trade era.
1854–56		Crimean War. Florence Nightingale.	Armoured battleships.
1857		Indian Mutiny. Palmerston's death. Gladstone.	Development of Empire in Canada, S. Africa, N. Zealand, India and Australia. Charles Darwin's *Origin of Species.*
1870		Forster's Education Act. Disraeli, Suez Canal purchase.	Livingstone in Africa.
1884		General Gordon in Sudan.	Home Rule struggle in Ireland— Parnell.
1887		Imperial display at Jubilee.	Cecil Rhodes in S. Africa.

DATES	MONARCHS	EVENTS AND PEOPLE	BACKGROUND
1899–1902		Boer War— Ladysmith, Kimberley, Mafeking (1900) —Roberts and Kitchener.	1869, Boneshaker bicycle. 1878, Telephones in use. Motor cars on the roads. Dunlop tyres.
1901	Edward VII.	Liberals in office; Balfour.	Marconi and Oliver Lodge—wireless (1901).
1903		First Aeroplane Flight—Wrights.	Old Age Pensions (1908).
1910	George V.	Captain Scott (1912).	Suffragette movement. Popular Press.
1914–18		The Great War— 1914, Marne, Ypres, Falklands; 1915, Gallipoli, Loos, Nurse Cavell; 1916, Verdun, Jutland, Somme, Lloyd George; 1917, U-boats, U.S.A. enters war, Russian Revolution, Allenby and Lawrence; 1918, Foch and Haig.	Emancipation of women. Development of Aircraft. Conscription and Rationing. Use of tanks.
1919		League of Nations.	Social Unrest. Coal Strike 1921.
1921		Irish Free State.	1926, General Strike. 1929–33, mass unemployment.

DATES	MONARCHS	EVENTS AND PEOPLE	BACKGROUND
1931		Statute of Westminster—Empire into Commonwealth.	
1936	Edward VIII. George VI.		Television—Baird.
1939–45		Second World War. Winston Churchill.	Education Act, 1944.
			United Nations, 1946.
1947		India's Freedom.	Fear of Russia.
			Festival of Britain, 1951.
1952	Elizabeth II.		
1957		Ghana became self-governing.	Nationalism in Africa.
1960		Nigeria independent.	
1961		S. Africa left the Commonwealth.	First space flight.

A SHORT INDEX